Early praise for Chris Padgett's *Wholly Mary: Mother of God*

"Chris Padgett brings a welcome invasion of the reality of Mary into the intimacy of your own home. Rediscover how Mary is not only relevant but essential in the Church, the world, and your personal, everyday life."

—Brad Farmer, cofounder, APeX Ministries,
Catholic evangelist

"The saints have often said that we can never have enough of Mary. In this book about Our Lady, Chris Padgett provides ample reason for why this is true. Written in a very personal style, I highly recommend this book for those who desire to know and love Our Lady in a more personal way!"

—Fr. Donald Calloway, M.I.C., author of *No Turning Back: A Witness to Mercy*

WHOLLY MARY

WHOLLY MARY

MOTHER OF GOD

CHRIS PADGETT

SERVANT
BOOKS

PUBLISHED BY ST. ANTHONY MESSENGER PRESS
CINCINNATI, OHIO

Cover and book design by Mark Sullivan
Cover image © PunchStock | Photodisc

ISBN 978-0-86716-977-5

LIBRARY OF CONGRESS CATALOGING-IN-PUBLICATION DATA
Padgett, Chris, 1970-
Wholly Mary, Mother of God / Chris Padgett.
p. cm.
Includes bibliographical references (p.   ).
ISBN 978-0-86716-977-5 (alk. paper)
1. Mary, Blessed Virgin, Saint—Theology. 2. Mary, Blessed Virgin, Saint—Devotion to. 3. Catholic Church—Doctrines. I. Title.
BT613.P33 2011
232.91—dc22
2011010315

Published by Servant Books,
an imprint of St. Anthony Messenger Press.
28 W. Liberty St.
Cincinnati, OH 45202
www.AmericanCatholic.org
www.ServantBooks.org

Printed in the United States of America.
Printed on acid-free paper.
11 12 13 14 15   5 4 3 2 1

To Jesus:

Accept this little homage of the love I bear Thee and Thy beloved Mother. Do Thou protect it by showering down on all that read it the light of confidence and flames of love towards this Immaculate Virgin in whom Thou hast placed the hope and whom Thou hast made the refuge of all the redeemed. And as a reward for my poor labor, grant me, I beseech Thee, that love towards Mary, which, by the means of this book, I desire to see enkindled in all that read it.

— St. Alphonsus de Liguori, *The Glories of Mary*

To all the lovely women in my life
—Hannah, Sarah, Madeline, and Mary Padgett—
and especially my wife, Linda.

I also know that my boys
—Noah, Kolbe, Jude, and Joseph—
need to foster their devotion to Mary, too.

With thanks to Lucy Scholand and Servant Books,
for making my run-on sentences
not run on so long.

CONTENTS

INTRODUCTION

O Lady, protect me in my struggles and strengthen me
when I am beginning to waver.
—François-Louis Blosius

I have been blessed with very strong women in my life. Both my
maternal and paternal grandmothers were loving and truly matri-
archal.

I can honestly say that when I visited my grandmother on my
father's side, I was certain to have the best time of my life. She
loved to celebrate, loved to laugh, and it seemed her whole day
would revolve around whatever my sister and I could possibly
dream of doing. We would stay up late playing cards, telling stories I'd heard countless times before, and talking about what we
might do in the coming days together. Everything could become
the greatest of adventures with her.

One summer I stabbed myself in the foot with a lawn dart and,
yes, I was probably the reason that game was discontinued. There
was bloodshed, along with weeping and gnashing of teeth.

Grandmother was there with Epsom salts, the television at the ready, and plenty of sweets to get me through this difficult time.

There were downsides to Grandma Phyllis's protective instincts. Often it was said that none of the females dating or marrying her boys were ever good enough. Her commitment to them was that complete.

My maternal grandmother was very different but no less loving. Arda Perkins was a faith-filled woman who prayed constantly for her family, cherished the Scriptures, and never missed a Sunday as far as I knew. I gained from her the knowledge that no matter how difficult life could be, following Christ was all that mattered. I think Grandma Arda would consider her job complete if all the children she ever cared for held Jesus close to their hearts.

I have a lot of stories about Grandma Arda, many of them centering on the fact that she was blind. She was fearless when it came to her handicap, demonstrating independence by entering dozens of Senior Olympics, tobogganing, waterskiing, and strolling about the suburbs of Detroit with only her Seeing Eye dog. Everyone who met Grandma Arda was inspired.

Yet her voice was one of the worst I've ever heard. And she put that voice to use every morning by waking us up with her rendition of "School Days." None of us could sleep through that. And her laugh would almost certainly qualify as a cackle.

These two grandmothers showed me an unintended yet profound picture of the Blessed Mother. Mary would certainly have made the home in Nazareth a safe haven of joy and celebration. It's not hard to imagine neighbor kids flocking there to enjoy food, laughter, and toys from the carpentry shop. I am sure Mary made each child feel welcome. I am also confident that when she looked at her child, there was no one else who could compare.

Mary, too, was a great woman of faith. We can assume that she prayed continually and was fearless amid great obstacles. Any who came into her presence would certainly have seen that there was something unique about this woman, that she was absolutely "blessed…among women" (Luke 1:42)! And even now she longs to see all in her family, which includes us, love God with complete devotion. Her job isn't done until we are all with Jesus in heaven, holding him close to our hearts.

Really, Mary best demonstrates the human element of maternity—the best our wives, mothers, sisters, grandmothers, and daughters can offer. She is that perfect place of safety, acceptance, and growth. She carries none of the flaws that our own feminine examples do—none of the distraction, sin, or confusion concerning the maternal role. And so she offers our times a bulwark of consistency in devotion and fearless faithfulness.

We must resist the temptation to shuffle Mary into a corner, thinking her to be so meek and mild as to be paralyzed by the horrors of our modern age. Possibly we can't see how she could relate to our everyday lives of business and familial obligations. With only one child, who was perfect, and a husband who was almost perfect, how hard could life have been for her, right?

If we hold to this idea of Mary, we do the Blessed Mother a great disservice. The Church has a rich heritage of devotion to her. This attentiveness is not an obligatory means of getting Jesus to hear us better or a way to impress our priests or someone in our family. Marian devotion is not something we should force on ourselves and our families; neither is it something to ignore.

So what is Marian devotion all about? Why should we care about Mary? And if we do have reason to know more about her, what is the best way to approach this subject? Hopefully this book will help answer these questions.

I encourage you to approach this topic with a fresh perspective. Perhaps you have received misinformation about Mary that has limited or skewed your understanding of her. Perhaps you've encountered people devoted to Mary who seem, to put it bluntly, odd. If you can revisit this topic with an open heart, I am confident you will be surprised at the role Mary has played in the Church and what that can mean for you.

Mary isn't only about information; rather she is cheering us on and assisting us as we are transformed into the image and likeness of her son. She is truly a mother concerned about her children. So let's investigate this subject with openness and with a solid eye on where we have been as a Church in devotion to Mary, where we are individually in understanding her role for us and others, and where we are heading.

Would that all of you could have met my grandmothers. But how much better to introduce you to the woman who has all their good qualities to the max and none of their foibles. Let's get started.

CHAPTER ONE

A Few Basics

God created the heavens and the earth and, out of his great love, man and woman in his image and likeness. The human person was not a surprise but rather a specific intention on the part of the Divine Trinity. Thankfully we know from Scripture and Church teaching that he has been interested in every one of us from the very beginning. That is pretty profound when you consider the fact that God doesn't need us to exist in order to satisfy some emptiness or longing of his; rather he chooses our existence because of complete gratuitousness, the fecundity between the Trinity of persons. God is actually interested in us!

When we look at the story of how God has invited his creation into dialogue and friendship with him, we can begin to realize that he wants more than just lip service from us; he wants complete self-donation. The perfect model for this is Jesus, who gave himself over consistently to the will of the Father in the love of the Holy Spirit. Because of Jesus' life, death, and resurrection, we are all God's children through baptism. This is radical spirituality: God invites his creation into unfathomable intimacy.

So now that you are in the family of God, you should begin to grow into the reality of what that means. One of the amazing things about this heavenly family is that you have a mother who will guide you. She is the same mother Jesus had, and she will do everything possible to bring you into conformity with her son. In other words, you get what he got: the Father, who is watching and guiding you, and Mary as your mother, who will walk with you on your mission to please God.

God's love for his creation extends to you, and in freedom you can either respond favorably to this love or pursue yourself. You can do what you know is right, or you can follow your cravings into areas that you know will not please God.

Sometimes we want to do the good but struggle to actually do it. This sounds like St. Paul in Romans 7:15: "I do not understand my own actions. For I do not do what I want, but I do the very thing I hate." Yet look at how far St. Paul went in his sanctity, even though he struggled with his wants and desires.

There is hope for all of us. And Our Lady models best for us what it means to love her son. Knowing her and getting her help will enable you to become the saint you've been created to be.

Marian devotion is not just another task that needs to be checked off on the day's "to do" list; rather it is an opportunity to realize you have a mother who is waiting for you to get to know her son more and longs to assist you in doing so. I'm sure you already realize that moms have a way of getting what they want, and what Mary desires is for her children to be entirely devoted to her son, our brother Jesus Christ.

How to Be Holy

Have you heard stories about the great Catholic saints and thought, "I wish I could be like them"? Finding out that St. Francis could talk to animals, traveled great distances speaking of God's love (even to Sultan Malik al-Kamil in Egypt), and was given the stigmata (the wounds of Christ on his body) makes us want to have that type of connection with God, too. We hear about St. Maximilian Kolbe, who offered his life on behalf of a family man while imprisoned in Auschwitz, and wish that we could do heroic things like that for God. St. John Bosco loved young people and was given many visions and dreams. He also founded the Salesian order, which is still going strong today.

Maybe you like St. Clare, who gave away all she had in order to have Christ as her only treasure. At the end of her life, when she was very sick and couldn't attend Mass, the image of the priest praying Mass would be displayed upon her wall for her to see. So now she is the patron saint of television!

I love the saints. Their stories can be exciting, and they make me wonder what truly great things I could do for God. But when I look in the spiritual mirror, I realize that my life falls short of the heroism I see in these witnesses. I certainly don't have all of the cool supernatural powers that seem to come with being a follower of Christ. I do not heal the blind, levitate as did St. Teresa of Avila, bilocate as did Padre Pio, or run faster than a speeding bullet (oops, that was Superman). I don't carry on conversations with my guardian angel, as did St. Gemma Galgani, or hear instructions from saints of old, as did St. Joan of Arc.

Most of us have trouble getting up in the morning and being nice to our family members, so how could we really be saints? If only we were somebody else, like a nun or a priest—sanctity is easier for them. Well, not necessarily.

When reality sets in, I know that for me to be a saint, a great miracle has to occur. How can I be spiritually heroic when I struggle to do the small things in life? This is the big question for me, and I suspect it is for you, too.

We are all different from one another, and that makes our struggles unique, too. Even if we share the same spiritual weakness, our challenges are still particular to our situations in life. For example, I am married and have a lot of kids, so my journey toward sainthood will be different from that of a priest. That being said, there are some things we all can do in order to put the odds of living real sanctity in our favor.

The most important things we can do to be holy are probably easy for you to guess. We must become people of the sacraments and also nurture a true devotion to the Blessed Mother. The two complement each other, and they are guarantees for a healthy spirituality, regardless of our differences or commonalities.

The not-so-funny thing about this is that most people find Church a drag, the Eucharist a routine, confession scary, sacramental marriages a wreck, the priesthood under fire, death frightening, and devotion to Mary boring. Does that about cover it?

Great News

I do have some encouraging news for you. St. Thérèse of Lisieux (the Little Flower) was a young Carmelite nun who had something to say about what it means to really follow Jesus. The Little Flower was in a cloistered convent (a place of seclusion, enclosed, separate from the world) in France, and yet somehow she became a doctor of the Church! She didn't have CDs, T-shirts, books, or a television ministry, yet she has become for the Church a beautiful witness of holiness, offering teaching that is acknowledged to be of great importance.

St. Thérèse shows us that we can offer our small joys and even failures to Jesus as a gift. Her "little way" can be very encouraging for people like you and me, because it is proof positive that God isn't waiting for us to impress him with all sorts of awesome signs. What if the greatest sign you can do is give your little moments of joy and sorrow to Jesus as a gift? That gift, St. Thérèse says, can be enough to make you a great saint!

I think this is hard for many of us to believe. We feel that real sanctity involves doing something radical, like walking on water, making the lame walk, or rescuing small kittens from tall trees. St. Thérèse shows us that sanctity may not be so visibly extravagant. We can be heroic for God even if we are small in the world's eyes.

Blessed Mother Teresa of Calcutta is well known for her amazing work with the poorest of the poor, first in India and then in many other countries. Yet she, too, decided to do little things for God with great love. (Thérèse of Lisieux was her patron saint, by the way.) Mother Teresa could not cure the world of poverty and hunger, yet she could feed and love the child in her arms. And that amounted to an outstanding selflessness that impacted the world!

So even though you have your weaknesses and limited abilities, God wants to do something fantastic in and through you! I am sure you've heard this before, but God does have a wonderful plan for you. He is inviting you to become the saint that he has made you to be.

So how do we accomplish this awesome task of being God's saint? I've written another book on this topic, *A Spirituality You Can Live With*, and I hope you read that, too. But for now...

Even though we may be goofy and awkward, God really does want us to be completely given over to him. It is OK if we have difficulties, because he will help us overcome them. With this fact in mind, our call to be saints becomes very specific, in both its expression and our hurdles.

In other words, each saint's actual witness of intimacy with God is a very unique manifestation of what he wanted to do in and through that person. The same will be true for you. As you give yourself more and more to the love of God, you will manifest his life through your specific existence, amid your circumstances and struggles. He isn't giving up on you, and that should be reason enough to celebrate!

You don't have to be anything except who God created you to be. Maybe you won't be bilocating anytime soon, but you can take every moment and live for Christ right where you are. If you can walk on water, I am certain you'll gather a crowd, but that won't necessarily make you a saint. St. Paul said to the Corinthian church, "If I give away all I have, and if I deliver my body to be burned, but have not love, I gain nothing" (1 Corinthians 13:3). Wow! That is heavy!

Sanctity is all about giving our small gifts to Jesus in love. Amazing miracles, talents, and even martyrdom all have their place, but in order for them to be truly important for Christ and his kingdom, they have to be soaked in love.

What Do You Want?

Mary's whole life was soaked in love. She wanted the Father's will above all else. What do you want?

If you want a CD, you save your money and buy one. If you want a new dress, you steal your husband's checkbook—just joking. If you're a student and want good grades, you have to study. If you want to be on the varsity team—whether football, baseball, basketball, or bocce—you train, investing time and effort in the sport in order to achieve excellence. If you want to be in the Olympics, you will spend years, hours on end, training yourself to be the best in the world.

What is my point? It is that when you want something, you figure out how to get it, and then you go for it. And usually, if your mind is set on the task and your goal is reasonable, you can get what you want, even earthly and temporal things.

Now ask yourself this: What do I want spiritually? Do I want to be a saint? Do I want to change the world for Christ? If so, then it will happen. When you want what God wants, it is going to happen! (Fr. John Gordon, of Newark, New Jersey, told me this in confession once.) And the beautiful truth is that God wants you to be a saint. He wants to empower you to change the world.

But the question remains: How does it all work? How do we live our faith in real situations?

God has done everything possible to make you the unique saint that our world needs right now. The only thing that is in your way is probably yourself. That seems funny to say, but it is true.

You have likely heard about the great oppositions to our faith: the world, the flesh, and the devil. They are real obstacles, but "we are more than conquerors through him who loved us" (Romans 8:37), and God "has granted to us all things that pertain to life and godliness" (2 Peter 1:3). "The God and Father of our Lord Jesus Christ…has blessed us in Christ with every spiritual blessing in the heavenly places" (Ephesians 1:3). And "he who is in you is greater than he who is in the world" (1 John 4:4). All of these wonderful Scriptures point out that you have been called and prepared to run this race with excellence!

I hope you are a little excited, because being in the family of God is never boring!

Some people don't know this. You can't imagine how many times I have run into people who tell me that their religious training was an agony. It takes real skill to make the Scriptures boring! Think about it: We see death, murder, adultery, deception, betrayal, talking animals, sibling rivalry, awesome miracles, great kings, battles, snakes, bears, prophets, and angels crammed into the Old Testament and even cooler things in the New. The Bible is packed with everything you could want in an adventure story, with the greatest of endings! Maybe if it were titled *Lord of the Universe*, with a cool cover, more people would check it out.

Living for God is exciting stuff, my friends, and we have the chance to bring this adventure into our homes and any other place we go.

What About Mary?

I bet you're wondering when we'll get to the specifics about Mary. I have not talked much about her, and this little book is supposed to center on why we should be excited about all that the Church has proclaimed concerning Our Lady. But the more you get excited about Our Lady, the more you'll get excited about being a saint. And the more you grow in holiness, the more you'll want to know Our Lady.

Now that that's settled, let's go back to those two things we find in the life of every canonized saint. The first is the important place of the sacraments, and the second is a great love for the Blessed Mother. If you really want to be a saint, changing the world with Christ's love, then you must have a deep and abiding love for Mary.

What do you think of when someone says, "Let's all pray the rosary"? Many of us probably envision ourselves being bored to death. Getting excited about Mary just seems old-fashioned, like a chance for old people to be part of a club or a gang. Can you see it, a dozen seniors dressed in leather and armed with shiny rosaries, surrounding a movie theater?

Some people see praying the rosary or wearing a scapular as a sort of good luck charm rather than anything substantial and worthwhile. I think of those people who get freaked out while staring at a Mary statue or picture, maybe thinking, "Are the eyes following me?"

Many people truly wonder how the Virgin Mary fits into their real life. Does she care about laundry, diapers, plays, concerts, or any of the other events that we find so important? How does being excited about Mary really help us follow Christ?

Maybe you have had bad experiences with Marian devotion, and these seem to get in the way of any real relationship with her. Maybe your parents forced you to pray the rosary, even though you felt as if you got nothing out of it. Possibly your perspective on the Blessed Mother is distorted because your earthly mother hasn't demonstrated loving characteristics.

Whatever the obstacle is between you and Mary, I want you to know that God works through that struggle with you. He has given you Mother Mary to help bring you into the fullness of your calling. It is safe to say that the more your relationship with her deepens, the more you will become the great saint God wants you to be.

If God has gone to such effort to share the Blessed Mother with us (Jesus gave her to us from the cross, John 19:26–27 tells us), then surely we have reason to investigate further her role in our lives. So let's find out more about this person who is our spiritual mother.

CHAPTER TWO

Mary the Woman

In order to understand the depths of Our Lady's maternal impact, we must start with who she was two thousand years ago. She was a woman within a specific society and culture, the nation of Israel. And that takes us to our Bibles.

Studying Scripture can be a lot of fun, but sometimes it is difficult to understand what certain passages mean. The Church helps us understand the Word of God. One proven formula that protects the student from a false interpretation is to understand the senses of Scripture. We apply the literal and historical method—which addresses the genre and what the text actually says—before unfolding the spiritual sense, which are the allegorical, moral, and anagogical meanings. Basically, if you find the literal meaning first—that is, what the author intended to say—then the spiritual will be better understood.

The *Catechism of the Catholic Church* offers further principles for understanding Scripture: First, we must be aware of its content and unity (see *CCC*, #112). We as a Church are the recipients of the deposit of faith, which Christ gave to the apostles. What we understand about our spirituality must fit within the dimensions of who we are as his body.

Certain books within sacred Scripture seem to contradict others, yet this cannot be, since the primary author of the whole of Scripture is God, and he cannot contradict himself.[1] The Bible is inspired, or "God-breathed." It is because of this that the individual books cannot be pitted one against the other. Sacred Scripture is a cohesive whole, and we must keep in mind what God has said in the Old Testament in order to see the beauty of development in the New (see *CCC*, #128–129).

Second, we are to note the living tradition of the whole Church. "According to a saying of the Fathers, Sacred Scripture is written principally in the Church's heart rather than in documents and records, for the Church carries in her Tradition the living memorial of God's Word, and it is the Holy Spirit who gives her the spiritual interpretation of the Scripture ('according to the spiritual meaning which the Spirit grants to the Church')" (*CCC*, #113, quoting Origen, *Homily in Leviticus 5, 5*: PG 12, 454D). What we understand about Mary in Scripture is therefore consistent with the Church's understanding of her role and maternity.

And finally we acknowledge the analogy of faith. Mark Shea says that this refers to "those doctrinal statements that summarize and symbolize what we believe."[2] The *Catechism* says, "By 'analogy of faith' we mean the coherence of the truths of faith among themselves and within the whole plan of Revelation" (*CCC*, #114).

In looking at Marian Scripture passages, we want to follow the Church's guidance. So I've included here some quotes from Catholic scholars, popes, and Vatican II to help us understand what God has to say about this holy woman.

A Devout Jew

One thing we notice in looking at women during Jesus' time is that they were almost always wives and mothers. Back in the old days—actually the really old days, when Mary was young—Jewish women were usually given in marriage and expected to become mothers. That was their responsibility and an opportunity for them to be provided for. "He gives the barren woman a home, / making her the joyous mother of children" (Psalm 113:9).

Bearing children was an important honor, because it continued the family line. And many a Jewish woman hoped to bring forth the promised Messiah. The people of Israel were tired of being in captivity and longed for God's promised deliverer.

We first encounter Mary as a young woman betrothed. Betrothal in those days was a different arrangement from what we see today. Fr. Richard Batey writes:

> Betrothal in Israel, as among other nations, was a far more serious contract than are present-day engagements. During the approximate year between the betrothal and nuptial ceremonies, the betrothed girl was legally the man's wife even though she was still a virgin, since the marital relation did not begin until the nuptial ceremony. The betrothal could be abrogated only by a formal written divorce or death.[3]

Mary was to be a wife and mother, but she was also a virgin. This definitely set her apart. Are there any examples in the Scriptures of people abstaining from marital relations? In the book *The Virgin Mary,* Jean Guitton looks at a few occasions for celibacy, and all the exceptions to the rule of marriage were men.

> It has been observed that, when Mary lived, there were certain currents in religious thought that were favorable to virginity. In the case of some outstanding religious mission, the Jews conceded, to men, the right to renounce marriage: Elias, Eliseus, Jeremias, John the Baptist—none of these ever married. This impressed the people as something of which they themselves were incapable. And there were the Essenes, too, who undertook to forgo marriage.[4]

Even for the married there were occasions for abstinence, especially for those destined to have encounters with God. The Levitical priests, when entering the Holy of Holies, and also the faithful going on pilgrimage to Jerusalem were called to prepare themselves by abstinence. So the Catholic teaching about celibacy and even periods of abstinence has some historical basis in Scripture.

Virginity gained momentum in Christian spirituality over time, especially as the message of Christ spread throughout the world. Mary, as virgin and mother, established a model the Church has strived to follow in her purity and holiness on its great pilgrimage of faith.

> The consecrated life has always been seen primarily in terms of Mary—Virgin and Bride. This virginal love is the

source of a particular fruitfulness which fosters the birth and growth of divine life in people's hearts. Following in the footsteps of Mary, the New Eve, consecrated persons express their spiritual fruitfulness by becoming receptive to the Word, in order to contribute to the growth of a new humanity by their unconditional dedication and their living witness.[5]

Why would Mary want to be a virgin?

Mary had the most incredible encounter with God of all time, and some might speculate that that alone could be why she longed for virginity. The Annunciation and Incarnation far surpassed Abraham's call from God, Moses' encounter in the burning bush and later at Mount Sinai, and the Levitical priests' service in the Holy of Holies. Our Lady became the tabernacle of God, the living ark of the covenant! She far surpasses the Old Testament witnesses to abstinence in that she carried the Divine inside of her for nine months!

There is general consensus, however, that Mary took a vow of virginity at a very young age, well before the Annunciation. Scripture does not indicate how she planned to demonstrate this consecration to the Father but nevertheless hints at its actuality. To become a mother was not something Mary had assumed, and so she asked how the Lord would bring to fruition his will. Her question did not stem from unfamiliarity with reproductive techniques; rather she clearly had given her body to God as a gift and intended a life of singular devotion both in body and soul.

Wife and Mother

How was Mary to live her vocation in the Jewish society of her time? Jean Guitton states:

> Mary could not have thought she would go on living at home without marrying: such a status was unknown in her time. She must, therefore, have envisaged marrying. It must be clearly understood that, in a society in which virginity was unknown and unsafeguarded (for there was no institution to preserve it, no model to consecrate it), Mary's vow could not be accomplished except in the married state. For her, marriage was a necessity: it was only through marriage she could achieve her design: in marriage alone could she keep her virginity.[6]

It is realistic to assume that this woman of great faith believed that God would bring her a spouse who would honor her vow. "She must have reasoned: 'God would never contradict himself. If he has prompted my vocation, he must also have ordered the sequence of events that can make it possible. He will have inspired in the man I happen to wed a disposition corresponding to my own.'"[7]

It has been popular to view St. Joseph as old and beyond any interest in matters physical, but this does a great disservice to the integrity, chastity, and love he had for Mary.

> [W]e are asked to believe that Mary had no love, in the ordinary sense, for Joseph, but saw in him a mere protector, a shield to cover from human eyes what was about to be accomplished in her womb. Similarly, we are to suppose

that Joseph's love for Mary was purely patriarchal: she was
just a child entrusted to his care. In neither relation is there
any authentic love.[8]

Mary and Joseph were betrothed before the Annunciation, and
the Church holds that this was certainly more than a marriage of
convenience. True, Joseph would supply the Davidic lineage to
the Christ child and care for the family materially. Yet his reception of the angel's messages indicates a man of spiritual strength
and determination. In fact, the love within the Holy Family was
singular and unlike anything the world had previously seen; we
could say that it was the most authentic familial love the world
had ever witnessed.

Scholars have found in St. Joseph a figure far more heroic than
we might have previously imagined. Let us settle on these words
from Guitton:

Joseph's love could have been unbounded, not to be
expressed in words, fierce as a torrent, calm, smooth and
unruffled as a lake, fresh as springing water. He no doubt
perceived in this girl an affinity to himself; but he would
have felt her superiority. A man's love moulds itself on that
of the woman; hers to guide quietly the impulse of the
man. It was Mary who bestowed on Joseph the gift of virginity, as she was to bestow it with her smile on countless
young men, and on the worldwide race of priests, whom
she enables to preserve so easily their manly virginity. Yet
she took from him nothing of his natural vigor, nothing of
his zest and fervor; she diminished nothing of his capacity
to give and receive tenderness. The eyes of Joseph were

changed through meeting hers; his senses were sublimated, caught as they were in the radiance of that body unique in all the world. Here was a strange and peaceful moment, recalling the first love in the first days of the world: the love of Adam and Eve, both of them virgin before they sinned.[9]

My heart resonates with Guitton's perspective of St. Joseph as a man's man. I am also struck by the insight that Mary's proclivity toward God transformed Joseph. He would in fact be that man who would love her truly yet be of like mind in giving himself to the will of God as the masculine counterpoint of her self-donation. Theirs was an authentic marriage, with joy and laughter, stories and delight.

Basic family life for Mary would have been similar to that of other faithful Jewish families. The wife would perform the full round of domestic duties, while the husband would work a trade. The virtuous wife, Scripture tells us, "looks well to the ways of her household, / and does not eat the bread of idleness" (Proverbs 31:27).

It was rare for a woman to study religion, yet a familiarity with the Jewish faith would be expected. Pilgrimages would be taken; children would be dedicated at the temple and nursed for an average of eighteen months. If the child were a boy, the name would be given on the eighth day when he was circumcised. Women attended synagogue, prayed toward the temple three times a day during sacrifice, and listened to the homilies of the rabbi. (Even though women were separate from men in the synagogue, they would hear the catechesis.)

Mary certainly experienced all of this, and in a heightened manner due to her intimate relationship with the Trinity. She was like a sponge soaking up everything she could about the God of Abraham, Isaac, and Jacob.

What is uncommon about the Holy Family is that Mary and Joseph were favored with caring for and nurturing the God-man in the most intimate of ways. Whereas Moses climbed the mountain to converse with God on behalf of the people, Mary gazed into the face of the God-man every day. The beauty of self-donation within the Holy Family is an inspiration for us today.

We have much more to learn about Mary. Here we begin to see that she was a real person, living in a real city with neighbors, customs, and cultures. Her vocation was unique, as were her challenges.

Mary's Gift

"What is man that thou art mindful of him?" (Psalm 8:4).

From the very beginning of time, man has longed for answers to primordial questions. What are we here on earth for? Why is there suffering, and what happens when we die? The Church recognizes these questions as common to all:

> Men look to their different religions for an answer to the unsolved riddles of human existence. The problems that weigh heavily on the hearts of men are the same today as in the ages past. What is man? What is the meaning and purpose of life? What is upright behavior, and what is sinful? Where does suffering originate, and what end does it serve? How can genuine happiness be found? What

happens at death? What is judgment? What reward fol-
lows death? And finally, what is the ultimate mystery,
beyond human explanation, which embraces our entire
existence, from which we take our origin and toward which
we tend?[10]

God has been showing himself to man from the very beginning,
first through natural law but specifically in divine revelation, cul-
minating in the fullness of his revelation in Jesus Christ.[11] And
how did Jesus become revealed? The Second Person of the
Blessed Trinity became flesh and dwelt among us through this
Mediterranean woman.

Because of the Incarnation we are able to see what the love of
God truly looks like. Mary brings us love and helps us understand
love. She is the place where heaven touches earth.

. . .

CHAPTER THREE

Mary and the Trinity

In order for us to discover how Marian devotion can make a difference in our lives, let's look at her relationship with the Trinity.

Mary interacts with God in a way that we can barely fathom. She had a direct connection with God from the moment of her conception. And at the Incarnation the Creator willingly became dependent upon his creature.

Mary was favored by God more than all of creation in that she was chosen to mother, love, and collaborate with the mission of her Son as he did the Father's will in the love of the Holy Spirit.

> Was there ever a creature that the Trinity dealt more intimately with than Our Blessed Lady? Daughter of the Father, Mother of the Son, and Spouse of the Holy Spirit, she is the route God took to make his Son incarnate. She it is who 'leaves His light sifted to suit our sight' and for that makes Christians ever after anxious to pay her honor.[1]

Daughter of the Father

We understand God's fatherly heart by examining the way that he showed himself to the children of Israel. They were guided by the Lord through his prophets from captivity into the Promised Land, and when they wandered off in disobedience, he reproved them as a father does his child. The history of God's relationship with these chosen people shows progress from a family to a tribe to a nation to a kingdom.[2]

God chose to enter into covenant with Abraham, guaranteeing that his descendants would multiply beyond the stars in the sky (see Genesis 12:2–3; 15:5). The children of Abraham, Isaac, and Jacob carried within them a holy calling. The Creator set them apart to be the elder brothers within the family of God.

Mary realized that she was part of this tradition among the people of faith. "He has helped his servant Israel," she proclaimed in her prayer of praise, "in remembrance of his mercy, as he spoke to our fathers, to Abraham and to his posterity for ever" (Luke 1:54–55).

As a young Jewish woman, Mary committed her whole being to the service of the Father's will, desiring to please him in all things. Pope Paul VI wrote: "She, in fact, among human beings, offers the most shining example and the closest to us, of that perfect obedience whereby we lovingly and readily conform with the will of the eternal Father."[3]

When people talk about you, do they note how your life is centered on the things of God? Do they see in you a person who is interested in pleasing God in every part of your life? Those who knew Mary were not confused about where her heart was.

Mary knew the Father; she knew she could trust him with her whole life. She told the angel, "Behold, I am the handmaid of the Lord; let it be to me according to your word" (Luke 1:38).

Mother of the Son

The Son of God is Jesus. We know from Scripture that he was "born of woman" (Galatians 4:4). That woman was Mary. Her relationship with her son is profound. The incarnation of the God-man is forever associated with her generous assent. God's presence is now seen in Jesus, the Second Person of the Blessed Trinity.

Mary is the Mother of God (see chapter four on the Church's definitive dogma on this). She was also the first person who was fully redeemed, "in a more exalted fashion."[4] Having been preserved from original sin, Mary freely chose to submit in word and deed to the will of God, which culminated in mothering Jesus. She was the true disciple of Christ, learning from her Lord, and paradoxically she was his educator.

Mary fully assists her Son in his salvific mission. She is his handmaid, associate, and "mediatrix."[5] The relationship Mary has with the Second Person of the Blessed Trinity is greater than any human being has ever experienced. She is the icon for those following Christ, and her maternity extends to those who are his body.

What is Christianity all about? It is all about Christ! Mary is the one who knows Jesus best. She would probably sing to him at night and rock him to sleep. Consider how many times she gave Jesus a hug, a cup of water, or a toy to play with. Think of all the stories she could tell you of how he loved to play in the mud, jump in puddles, or swim in the river. She knew his favorite foods; she knew if he liked to sleep in late or get up early. She was with him in a singular way for thirty-three years! Surely we can learn much from her about her son.

Mary really loved Jesus as a mother but also believed in him as a disciple. Remember when she was with Jesus at Cana? She brought the lack of wine to his attention and encouraged the disciples to do whatever Jesus instructed (see John 2:5). What good advice for all of us! She stood by Jesus at Calvary, while other disciples fled. What a model of enduring love for the Master!

Spouse of the Holy Spirit

Mary's relationship with the Holy Spirit is unique as well. She was overshadowed by the Holy Spirit at the Annunciation, an event more profound than that of the glory cloud filling the temple in the Old Testament (see Exodus 40:34–35). She is truly the Spouse of the Holy Spirit.

St. Maximilian Kolbe, who had a strong devotion to Our Lady, wrote to a fellow priest:

> The Holy Spirit is in Mary after the fashion, one might say, in which the Second Person of the Blessed Trinity, the Word, is in his humanity. There is, of course, this difference: In Jesus there are two natures, divine and human, but one single person who is God. Mary's nature and person are totally distinct from the nature and person of the Holy Spirit. Still, their union is inexpressible, and so perfect that the Holy Spirit acts only by the Immaculata, his spouse.[6]

The Spirit of God fashioned Mary to mother the Christ child. He poured out on her the fullness of grace in light of her calling and maternal vocation. She was in the Upper Room when he empowered the Church to build the kingdom of God. "Mary's eminent sanctity was not only a singular gift of divine liberality. It was also the fruit of the continuous and generous cooperation of her free will in the inner motions of the Holy Spirit."[7]

Do you want the Spirit to come upon you in a fresh way? You need the Spirit to be a true saint. Mary can draw you into a deeper relationship with him and so help release his gifts in your life.

One With God

St. Bonaventure wrote of the eternal Father loving the eternal Son in the fullness of the Holy Spirit. The Son eternally gives all back to the Father in the love of the Holy Spirit. What does this Trinitarian exchange of complete self-donation look like for us in time?

> ... Using the logic of perfection of Anselm, [Bonaventure] applies this principle [that the Good is self-diffusive] in a general way to God claiming that God must contain the fullness of self-diffusion. But this cannot be realized in God's outpouring of himself in creation since creation is too limited to sustain the full force of the divine fecundity; it is like a mere speck in relation to the immensity of the divine goodness. Therefore this diffusion must be realized in the Trinity, where for all eternity there can be actualized

the fullest expression of fecundity in the Trinitarian processions.

Although the divine fecundity is not dependent on the world for its actualization, the world itself is an overflow and an expression of this fecundity. When the Father generates the Son, he produces in the Son the archetypes or rationes aeternae of all he can create.... Thus the Son is the link between the divinity and creation; for all of created reality is the expression of him and refers back to him.... [8]

The word *glory*, or a similar derivation, is noted throughout both the Old and New Testament. Jesus is very intent on giving glory to the Father (see John 8: 49–50; 12:28; 14:13; 15:8); this is primary in his actions. The Redemption expresses this glorification that is due to the Father.

Mary participates with Jesus in giving glory to God the Father. In fact, Mary did this perfectly. How can we imitate her in this beautiful display of devotion to and adoration of the Trinity?

First, we say yes to God's choosing to glorify himself in our smallness. He intends us in our humanity to be completely given over to Christ. We must develop a fertile spirit, in which the true vine might be planted and grow to fruition. Mary did just that. She said yes in a way that changed everything.

Second, we must be willing to join in the passion of Christ, placing our sufferings and sorrows in him for the redemption of sinners. In this we imitate Mary, who accepted the sorrows prophesied by Simeon as the Father's will. She united her heart to the heart of Jesus for the purpose of God—that none might be lost.

God has invited us on a wonderful adventure. He is excited about loving in and through us, even if we feel insignificant and unable to do great things for him. Consider Mary, the humble young woman of Nazareth, empowered by her relationship with the one true God—Father, Son, and Holy Spirit.

My soul magnifies the Lord,
and my spirit rejoices in God my Savior,
for he has regarded the low estate of his handmaiden.
For behold, henceforth all generations will call me blessed;
for he who is mighty has done great things for me,
and holy is his name.
And his mercy is on those who fear him
from generation to generation.
He has shown strength with his arm,
he has scattered the proud in the imagination of their
    hearts,
he has put down the mighty from their thrones,
and exalted those of low degree;
he has filled the hungry with good things,
and the rich he has sent empty away.
He has helped his servant Israel,
in remembrance of his mercy,
as he spoke to our fathers,
to Abraham and to his posterity for ever. (Luke 1:46–55)

CHAPTER FOUR

Four Fabulous Dogmas

There are four major truths our Church teaches about Mary. We hold to these truths without wavering because they are part of the deposit of faith. We recognize that Mary is

1. the Mother of God
2. ever Virgin
3. immaculately conceived
4. assumed into heaven

These are truths contained in divine revelation, which basically means that God shared this information with us. It is that important!

Most mothers are very protective of their children, and for good reason. Kids have a knack for hurting themselves or others. They seem to have an insatiable curiosity for things they are not supposed to get into. A mother's job can be pretty hard, especially for a child who is unhinged much of the time.

Mother Church takes care of us, even when we are in trouble. An example of that is her teaching about Mary. The Church knows that Mary protects the truth about Christ's nature. That is, everything the Church says about Mary derives from and supports what she tells us about Jesus. The more we know Mary, the better we can love her son.

So let's look at the Marian truths the Church presents in her teaching. Some of the words that are used may seem big and extravagant, but they're important, so I hope they sink in.

Theotokos: *Mother of God*

This first teaching is the most important when laying a foundation in Marian studies. It is the one Marian dogma that unites the others.

The first two centuries of Christianity were filled with drama unlike anything Hollywood could ever hope to capture and convey. What is so striking about this story of the Church is not the wars, expensive buildings, injustices, scandals, and dilemmas but the reality of its being the very body of Christ within time and history, despite the rough edges. Jesus remains on earth in a real way through the Church. This seems inconsistent, since we see so many blemishes in her, such as the arguments and sinful acts throughout history. Because of Christ the Church is spotless, even though many of its members could use a good cleansing!

The Church has encountered great oppositions and amazing successes. One of her adventurous moments involves the teaching about Mary as the Mother of God or *Theotokos*. The Council of Ephesus in 431 is important in this regard. It did not define a new teaching about Mary; rather it clarified a teaching about Jesus that some people had gotten confused.

Questions about who Jesus was are understandable. After all, Jesus was greater than natural boundaries (walking on water), stronger than supernatural realities (casting demons out), and a man of integrity and character (he didn't take the bread the devil offered him in the desert, for example). Was Jesus a man only, or was he God?

People could see that Jesus was a man because he was visible and known, but he also seemed beyond this world in his identification with the Father and his miraculous actions.

Jesus said he and the Father were one (see John 10:30) and even called himself I AM (Mark 14:61–62). This would mean something to the Jewish listeners, because that was the name of God that Moses had been instructed to proclaim to their ancestors enslaved by the Egyptians.

Quick point here: There is one God in three Persons—Father, Son, and Holy Spirit. You probably know this, but we always have to clarify that these are not different modes of expressing the one God; rather they are distinct Persons yet never separate. We call this dogmatic truth the Trinity.

Jesus, God the Son, is one Person with two natures, divine and human. We can't say that Jesus is just a man doing some pretty cool things. He is 100 percent God and 100 percent man, equaling 100 percent Person. (Math has always been difficult for me, but somehow I get this.) This is called the "hypostatic union."

Mary gave to Jesus his human nature, not his divine, but the two natures are never separate. The point of this is pretty important: Jesus is a Person with two natures, not two separate persons. His divine and human natures, although distinct, are never separate.[1] So Mary preserves in this title "Mother of God" the unity of Jesus' divinity and humanity within his one Person. She is the Mother of the whole Christ. A mother doesn't give birth to a soul or simply flesh; rather she delivers a person, both body and soul. Mary gave birth to Jesus, the Second Person of the Blessed Trinity, so she is the Mother of God.

I know this might be a bit heavy to take in all at once, so just imagine how hard it was for the early Church as she began trying to protect the true teaching about Jesus. Thankfully the Holy Spirit has ensured the proper teaching concerning the deposit of faith. But there were a lot of questions in the early Church, and some pretty serious mistakes were made by individuals and movements when it came to understanding who Jesus was and is.

The Council of Ephesus defined as dogma the teaching of *Theotokos*. Again, it is important to remember that a council does not create new doctrine; rather the bishops expound upon the already given deposit of faith and define more precisely what has been revealed. Mary, as the Mother of God, helped to clarify the reality of Christ's humanity. This was helpful in dealing with a heresy called Nestorianism.

The early Church recognized Mary as the Mother of God, and in many ways Mary was the icon the early Church followed as she strove to bring forth Christ into the world. Yet people wanted to know how the two natures of Christ were united. A priest named Nestorius wanted to teach that there were two persons: Christ the human, who had Mary as mother; and Christ who was God, divine, whom Mary could not mother.

At a Mass in Constantinople, during Advent of the year 408, a priest declared that Mary was not the Mother of God. This created a stir among the listeners. Later Nestorius echoed the priest: He said there were two persons in Christ and that Mary was mother of only the human one. His insistence upon this was problematic in that he was eventually consecrated bishop of Constantinople.[2]

St. Cyril, the patriarch of Alexandria, held that there was one God-man, with the unity of the two natures in this one Person. St. Cyril wanted to make sure that this was true, so he sent his Christology along with the Nestorian position to Pope Celestine for his discernment. The pope ruled in favor of Cyril's perspective and told Nestorius to amend his theology within ten days. The days passed, and Nestorius continued to proclaim his unapproved teachings on Christ and subsequently Mary. Cyril tried to stop Nestorius's error but to no avail.

The bishop of Rome called a synod in 430, at which Nestorius was told to recant, but he refused. Emperor Theodosius II decided to call a general council at Ephesus in 431 to have the matter definitively addressed and the concluding position enforced. The two parties, 160 bishops, gathered in Ephesus at the Church of Mary.

Many of Nestorius's supporters were late in arriving. It was hot, and after two weeks of waiting, the decision was made: Nestorius was officially condemned. When the people of Ephesus heard the verdict, they celebrated by shouting, *"Theotokos! Theotokos!"* Torches were lit, and the people escorted the bishops to their lodgings.

When the rest of Nestorius's party, led by John, the patriarch of Antioch, finally arrived, they would not embrace the council's decision. They organized a council of their own, which condemned Cyril of Alexandria and Memnon, the bishop of Ephesus. Things got pretty nasty, but eventually Nestorius was deposed to a monastery in Antioch, where he lived in exile.

Did you get all of that? Relax, there will not be a quiz. But I do suggest you review it when you have time, because this council has ramifications for Marian studies. Even though the dogmatic emphasis was Christological, the clarifying of his Person was in part due to the adamant stance of the Church on the dogma of the *Theotokos*. Clarifying the role of Our Lady does not take away from Christ's glory but rather proclaims it and helps to define and defend it.

The question should be asked, how does this matter to me?

History is bound to repeat itself, and certainly we see variations of a theme when it comes to heresy. There are even popular books today that promote theologies contrary to this and other Catholic dogmas. People are still questioning the Immaculate Conception and the perpetual virginity of Mary and distorting the reality of who Christ is. Many voices today demand our attention. The only one that matters is the Word, which was "in the beginning,…was with God," and is God (John 1:1). Knowing the Church's clear teachings on Christ and his mother should bring us peace.

We are not the inventors of this story. God started it by choosing to become incarnate through a woman. He could have done anything to implement his salvific plan, but he chose Mary to initiate this marvelous epic.

Ever Virgin

The Church says that Mary was a virgin before, during, and after the birth of Jesus. Does this seem like a weird teaching? What's wrong with sex in marriage?

I have friends who wonder why the Church insists upon this teaching. After all, marriage is a good thing (a sacrament, in fact), and having children is beautiful. So why insist that Mary remained a virgin after the birth of Christ?

What we have in the Blessed Virgin Mary is the living ark of the covenant. The original ark of the covenant was where God was present with the children of Israel (see Exodus 25:22). In it were the rod of Aaron, manna from the wilderness, and tablets with God's law written on them (see Exodus 13:33; 40:20; Deuteronomy 10:1–5; Hebrews 9:4). The ark of the covenant was holy and had to be kept undefiled. You may remember that Uzzah died after touching it, even though he was just trying to keep it from falling (2 Samuel 6:6–7)!

Mary bore within her the true Bread from heaven, the true priesthood, and the Word made flesh. These typological images are not accidental. They help us see Mary's perpetual virginity as a natural consequence of her containment of the Holy One.

Church fathers in the fourth century—such as Athanasius, Jerome, Augustine, and others—affirmed Mary's perpetual virginity. Augustine, bishop of Hippo and doctor of the Church, wrote: "He Who wrote on the tablets of stone without iron, made

Mary with child of the Holy Ghost; and He Who produced bread in the desert without ploughing, impregnated the Virgin without corruption; and He Who made the rod to bud without rain, made the daughter of David bring forth without seed."[3]

The Council of Constantinople II (553–554) referred to Mary as ever virgin two times. In 649 the First Lateran Council, under Pope St. Martin I, stated the dogmatic definition of the perpetual virginity of Mary. In 681 the Sixth Ecumenical Council accepted that previous council's teaching about Our Lady's perpetual virginity.

But why is this important? What does it mean for us?

The *Catechism* relates it to our own call:

> Participation in the divine life arises 'not of blood nor of the will of the flesh nor of the will of man, but of God' [*Jn* 1:13]. The acceptance of this life is virginal because it is entirely the Spirit's gift to man. The spousal character of the human vocation in relation to God [cf. 2 *Cor* 11:2] is fulfilled perfectly in Mary's virginal motherhood. (*CCC*, #505)

For many Protestants Mary's perpetual virginity appears to be a big problem. Passages in Scripture that speak about Jesus' brothers and sisters make it seem logical that Mary and Joseph had other children (see Matthew 12:46; 13:55; Mark 2:31–34; 6:3; Luke 8:19–10; John 2:12; 7:3, 5, 10; Acts 1:14; 1 Corinthians 9:5). The *Catechism* gives us this understanding:

> The Church has always understood these passages as not referring to other children of the Virgin Mary. In fact

James and Joseph, 'brothers of Jesus,' are the sons of another Mary, a disciple of Christ, whom St. Matthew significantly calls 'the other Mary' [*Mt* 13:55; 28:1; cf. *Mt* 27:56]. They are close relations of Jesus, according to an Old Testament expression [cf. *Gen* 13:8; 14:16; 29:15; etc.]. (*CCC*, #500)

Some early writers speculated that Joseph had children from a previous marriage, and many artistic renditions picture Joseph as an older man for that reason. But it is likely that such insights were written simply to preserve the integrity of Our Lady rather than as literal treatises concerning Joseph's marital history.

The Immaculate Conception

Some one hundred fifty years ago God chose to do something beautiful. A young girl in France had an encounter that was out of this world. Bernadette saw Our Lady several times, and these apparitions changed history. After asking the beautiful woman to identify herself, the young girl from Lourdes heard, "I am the Immaculate Conception."

In no way did Bernadette know about this specifically theological expression. She was a poor girl with little education, living in an age without technological access to the world's happenings. She didn't know that the Church had defined Mary as immaculately conceived on December 8, 1854.

This dogma is sometimes confused, even by cradle Catholics, with that of the Virgin Birth. That dogma we just discussed: Mary was a virgin before, during, and after the birth of Jesus. The dogma of the Immaculate Conception affirms that Mary was conceived without sin—that is, her soul did not bear the stain of original sin. Mary was not deprived of grace in any way from the moment of her conception.

The apostolic constitution of Pius IX *Ineffabilis Deus* says:

> When the Fathers and writers of the Church meditated on the fact that the most Blessed Virgin was, in the name and by order of God himself, proclaimed full of grace [Luke 1:28] by the Angel Gabriel when he announced her most sublime dignity of Mother of God, they thought that this singular and solemn salutation, never heard before, showed that the Mother of God is the seat of all divine graces and is adorned with all gifts of the Holy Spirit. To them Mary is an almost infinite treasury, an inexhaustible abyss of these gifts, to such an extent that she was never subject to the curse and was, together with her Son, the only partaker of perpetual benediction. Hence she was worthy to hear Elizabeth, inspired by the Holy Spirit, exclaim: "Blessed are you among women, and blessed is the fruit of your womb" [Luke 1:42].[4]

The apostolic constitution goes on to look at Mary as the new Eve and the lily among thorns.

So Mary is called "full of grace" by the archangel Gabriel, and the Church acknowledges this truth as part of the deposit of faith. What is the big deal about this dogma anyway? Let's go back to the beginning.

After Adam and Eve sinned in the Garden of Eden, we all became the recipients of original sin. What this means is that from the moment of conception, you and I are deprived of the

fullness of grace. That is what original sin is, a deprivation of
God's grace. When we are baptized, the Holy Spirit pours grace
into us, making us new creatures in Christ Jesus. Yet every one of
us born without the fullness of grace has given in to the tempta-
tions of the world, the flesh, and the devil. We allow concupis-
cence to become enflamed and then freely act upon what we
know to be offensive to God's will.

Mary was preserved from original sin because she was to
mother God in the flesh. This preservative redemption was still
totally dependent upon Jesus' salvific mission, but it was singular
in its application. The freedom was Mary's to live in a manner
worthy of this favor or to serve self. She acted upon the fullness
of grace in a way that pleased the Father, obviously preferring his
will to hers. She grew in this grace as she continued to choose
his will.

What scriptural foundation does the Church use in proclaim-
ing this teaching?

The Immaculate Conception is first seen in what is called the
protoevangelium or the "first gospel." The first Good News, found
in Genesis 3:15, speaks about the enmity between the Serpent
and its seed and the woman and her seed. *Enmity* is a word that
describes complete opposition, even hostility. Not for a moment
would the woman be in line with the Serpent's will, and this was
the first sign of hope given the primordial couple after they chose
self over God.

Mary is the Immaculate Conception because she was to be the
Mother of God. Just as the ark of the covenant, which bore God's
presence for Israel, was carefully and beautifully constructed

according to God's plan, so, too, is Our Lady. This gift she received from God was completely unearned.

In the Old Testament anyone sinful would be struck dead upon entering the Holy of Holies (see Leviticus 16:2). In fact, "only the high priest entered the inner room, and that only once a year, and never without blood, which he offered for himself and for the sins the people had committed in ignorance" (Hebrews 9:7). What does this say about Mary, who carried within her for nine months the very Word of God? The same Spirit who filled the temple of God came upon her. If there had been any sin upon her soul, she would have died. The preservative redemption our Lord extended to Mary was a beautiful expression of his generosity.

One other question that comes up about this dogma is this: If Mary is without sin, then why did Jesus have to come and die on the cross? We needed a perfect person to pay our debts to God; why couldn't Mary have done that?

The truth is, it took more than a person without sin to forgive our sins and restore grace to our lives. Our sin could not be forgiven by obedience or sinlessness alone; after all, that is what all of us are called to as his creatures anyway. The offense committed was against an eternal being, God. The recompense had to be repaid by one who was able to offer an eternal remedy. We really were up a creek without a paddle. If Jesus had not offered himself on Calvary, we could not be justified.

Our Lady's preservation from sin was for the glory of God the Son. She was chosen to mother God in the flesh, and her redemption was unique to her vocation. Remember how we talked about the fact that God calls each of us to be saints in a specific and unique way? So, too, with Mary.

The Church juxtaposes the Immaculate's obedience and Eve's disobedience: "By her obedience she became the new Eve, mother of the living" (*CCC*, #511). She is at enmity with the Serpent as she continues to crush his head on behalf of the Church. The blow she delivers is a mortal wound. We must not forget her maternal role in this great battle against the Serpent.

Mary does not seek attention; she does not want followers of Christ to see her as the focal point of devotion. She is the mother who wishes to lead us to a deeper intimacy with her son. God has given her to us—in order to protect, proclaim, and love us—and she does so perfectly.

The title Immaculate Conception speaks of Mary's office. The answer Mary gave Bernadette is not just a teaching but an introduction to her as a person, conceived without sin, who lived a life totally submitted to the Father's will. In light of her constant yes, we are privileged to invite her into our lives.

The Assumption

A little over fifty years ago, the Catholic Church made another definitive statement about the Blessed Mother. Not only is she the Mother of God, ever Virgin, and immaculately conceived, but Mary was assumed body and soul into heaven at the end of her life. Unlike our bodies, which will be put in the ground when we die, Mary's body has accompanied her spirit to heaven. She is bodily with her son right now, praying for us!

The 1950 proclamation of Mary's assumption into heaven was not a new doctrine by any stretch of the imagination. Indeed, countless churches already bore the name "assumption" or "dormition," the latter a term that refers to her "falling asleep," not dying. Rather the Church definitively declared the matter in response to questions about the end of Our Lady's life.

Because Mary is the Immaculate Conception, her body did not receive sin's effects, such as the decay of the body (*CCC*, #966, 974). The Church emphasizes this teaching, first, because it is true. Second, the teaching proves that we indeed have hope: God has given us a promise of spending eternity with him, and Mary witnesses to this promise. Her assumption into heaven says to everyone who is human (that includes you, by the way) that we do have the chance to be with Christ in heaven.

Remember, Jesus said that he goes to prepare a place for us (see John 14:2). St. Peter warns us not to grow weary of waiting, for Christ "is not slow about his promises as some count slowness" (2 Peter 3:9). Given our human weakness and what seems like a very lengthy delay, it is good to remind ourselves that the Blessed Mother is already where we hope to be!

We have relics of most of the saints—parts of their bodies, clothing they wore, things they touched. The veneration of relics is common and healthy, because they remind us of the saints and their witness and can even be means of healing and other spiritual favors (see Acts 19:12). With the love our Church has for Mary, if she had been buried in a tomb, surely we would have some relics of her to venerate. Yet there are none. Mary is already in heaven, body and soul.

Mary is praying for us. She knows us, loves us, and wants the best for us. Since she has been assumed into heaven, there hasn't been one moment when she has forgotten her children who are striving for holiness. She has her son's undivided attention and intercedes for greater strength in our spiritual lives. Even as the world seems to be falling apart, Mary's assumption extends to us the hope that we will spend eternity at the wedding feast of the Lamb.

The Point

I have discussed the main Marian teachings of our Church because they are the foundation for real devotion. We don't base our Marian devotion upon a feeling or a teaching that is "nice." We have seen the Church unfold Marian doctrines from the one deposit of faith, and knowing the Holy Spirit guides Christ's body, we can rest confident in the beauty of these truths for us today.

If we want to be like Jesus, we need to love Mary as our mother. If we want to know Jesus more, then we should ask Our Lady to teach us. If we want to be great saints for Christ, we need to depend on Mary, as the early Church and saintly heritage invite us to do.

When Gabriel visited Mary, it was to proclaim the coming Christ. When Mary visited Elizabeth, Christ was there. When the Magi found the child Jesus, he was with Mary. When Simeon, at the presentation of Jesus in the temple, testified about the mission and impact of this baby, Mary was there too, sharing in his story. When Mary realized at Cana that the wedding guests needed more wine, she mediated the need to the Lord (see John 2:3). Mary has always been about the will of her son and continues to be so in furthering our spiritual development.

Mary is our mother because Christ wishes this to be so. She will always guide us to her son, so that we, too, can be about his mission in the most effective way. She is the icon of true discipleship and the one the Church looks to as a model of real devotion. She is just waiting for us to ask for help in our pursuit of holiness.

CHAPTER FIVE

Trailblazer for Heroic Spirituality

Let's look a little further into the example Mary establishes for us in loving God.

As I mentioned earlier, she lived a life of devotion to God within her vow of virginity. Again, how this vow was demonstrated may never be fully understood, but it was certainly a complete gift of self. She was devoted to her son, even to the point of Calvary. Her way must become our path, since everyone following Christ must take up his or her cross (see Matthew 10:38).

Indeed, Mary has been in union with the Son from the beginning and remains faithful to his mission until the end. Vatican II tells us that even after she was assumed into heaven, "she did not lay aside [her] saving office but by her manifold intercession continues to bring us the gifts of eternal salvation."[1]

Partners in Salvation

In her very being Mary fulfills what was foreshadowed in the Old Testament: She is the saving ark, carrying within her the continuation of all that is Life. She is the faith of Abraham, trusting in the promise of God. She is the burning bush, which contains the Word of God and yet is untouched by harm. She is the new ark of the covenant, having within her the Word of God made flesh, the true prophet, and the real Bread from heaven.[2]

Mary is the great women of old, such as Judith and Esther, defeating the enemy through strength and intercession. And certainly Mary is found in the faith of Hannah, the devotion of Ruth, and the beloved in the Song of Songs. She is the virtuous woman of Proverbs 31 along with the daughter Zion.

Mary within her very self fulfills what were previously signs. She is the culmination of the early witness, and this is fitting for one who is Mother of God. From the beginning she is with her son. Her union continues to Calvary and Pentecost.

Because Mary is Mother of God, and in light of the fact that Christ as Head is not divided from his body, we can all call upon Mary as mother, too. She points the way for his body to offer itself to the Father.

It is a mystery, but Jesus Christ's one offering through the Spirit is salvific for us all. As blood and water poured from the side of Christ, we the Church were born. God's act of redemption in Christ shows us love in time. Real love became visible in its demonstration of self-sacrifice, and total gift in Jesus' oblation on Calvary.

Mary, through the Father's will, is allowed to offer her mother's heart, with and under Jesus, for the same purpose and intention as his, which is the redemption of the lost. Mary is part of Christ's active redemption. Her gift, by God's intention, becomes part of salvation history.

Each of us is invited to follow our spiritual mother's example, so we, too, can join in this redemption. We can become "a living sacrifice, holy and acceptable to God," by being "transformed by the renewal of [our] mind," to "prove what is the will of God, what is good and acceptable and perfect" (Romans 12:1–2).

Our participation in Christ's one sacrifice allows even our smallest sufferings to be united to the cross in a way that "fills up that which remains in Christ's sufferings" (Colossians 1:24). We are not uniting with Christ to remedy his offering, as if that offering somehow lacked potency in its application. This gift of Jesus to the Father in the love of the Holy Spirit is so great that it allows us as his body to participate in it.

I just love this stuff! You and I get to be a part of bringing people into a right relationship with God. Giving our all to God, as does Mary, is the greatest joy because it is what we were created to do: love God and love others.

Heroic Virtue

When we're talking about being saints, we have to talk about virtue. This is where the rubber meets the road, so to speak. The saints were first and foremost men and women of heroic virtue. Mary certainly exemplified this to the max. "She shines forth to the whole community of the elect as a model of the virtues."[3]

I'm sure Mary didn't wake up on the morning of the Annunciation with a sense that she needed her life to be a bit more devoted to God, in the hope of something special happening. She didn't visit Elizabeth just to gain favor with God by serving a family member. Virtue was part of her life, like breathing.

This is really a great model for all of us. We don't absent-mindedly pursue holiness, stumble upon a life of purity, or witness to a living faith without understanding. Your call and mine, for that matter, is to be a person living in the now! Saying yes to God's will in this moment will prepare us for potential great moments in the future. To be like the Blessed Mother is to be in the present tense, not fixated upon past mistakes or worried about future possibilities.

The *Catechism* defines virtue as "a habitual and firm disposition to do the good" (*CCC*, #1803). Doesn't that sound like something Mary had? Let's look at the theological virtues first—faith, hope, and love.

Certainly Mary was a woman of faith. "Let it be to me according to your word," she told the angel (Luke 1:38). And she "believed that there would be a fulfillment of what was spoken to her from the Lord" (Luke 1:45). Later she would not hesitate to approach Jesus with the wedding couple's need at Cana. Her continual yes to God and his plan is a loving response to God's fullness of grace, from her conception on into eternity.

"Hope is the theological virtue by which we desire the kingdom of heaven and eternal life as our happiness, placing our trust in Christ's promises and relying...on the help of the grace of the Holy Spirit" (*CCC*, #1817). It's keeping the eternal perspective in mind, especially when life hands us challenges.

Mary's life wasn't easy, you know. Even the Queen of Heaven and Earth went through some trials. Think of riding a donkey through the countryside when you're nine months pregnant—something we men can't begin to fathom. I would posit that the

Virgin Mary didn't hold a grudge against the innkeepers who could supply only a manger for the birth of the God-man. She would have delighted in showing them the hope of their redemption.

Mary is "our life, our sweetness, and our hope…in this valley of tears," as the *Salve Regina* prayer says. She is our model in seeing beyond the here and now to our eternal destiny in heaven. She exemplifies all that we hope to be and do for Christ.

And Mary prays for you, that you may have "the eyes of your hearts enlightened, that you may know what is the hope to which he has called you, what are the riches of his glorious inheritance in the saints, and what is the immeasurable greatness of his power in us who believe" (Ephesians 1:18–19).

As to the virtue of charity, Mary loves God "above all things for his own sake" (*CCC*, #1822), and she longs to let this intimacy overflow into each of us. She was and is an entire gift of love to family, friends, and strangers. She still wants to be with us, as evidenced by her repeated apparitions bringing wisdom, comfort, and healing to God's people. (See chapter twelve for more on this.)

I could go on and on about the virtues Mary manifested. We see her prudence in the fact that she pondered the holy happenings in her heart (see Luke 1:29; 2:51). We have already considered her obedience to God, but also notable is her obedience toward her husband, for she obeyed the direction that came from God through St. Joseph. And her chastity is an outstanding example of the virtue of temperance.

Obviously humility, which the *Catechism* calls "the foundation of prayer" (*CCC*, #2559), was hers. She knew who she was, "the handmaid of the Lord" (Luke 1:38). And she knew who God was—the Lord, her Savior, "he who is mighty" (Luke 1:46, 47, 49).

Mary is what we want to become. We want to hear and obey the Father's call. We desire to have Christ formed in us and to deliver him to those around us in need of salvation. We hunger to look, sound, and act like Jesus. Mary is our trailblazer for heroic spirituality. She shows us how to really be open to an encounter with God, which is what devotion to Our Lady highlights.

Reaching Back

A little over a year ago, my wife and I happened upon a wonderful opportunity to rent a small apartment just outside Rome. Due to my busy travel schedule, I'd collected a great quantity of frequent flyer miles, so I flew my mother up to Ohio and tricked her into watching the eight children while I took my "girlfriend" on a trip we'd never forget.

Linda and I arrived in Rome early that December, but our luggage didn't. This was quite a frustration for us, especially with the language barrier and no clear understanding of how to go about settling this difficulty. Ten days of traveling around Rome with only the clothes on our backs was not what we'd imagined. I kept thinking of the photos I would certainly take: Linda standing next to the Trevi Fountain, Linda in the Colosseum, Linda drinking espresso—all with the same shirt and pants on. It was one of those things that could be hilarious in retrospect but very discouraging at the time.

We left our cell number with the airline clerk, found a ride to our lodgings, and tried to stay awake long enough to counteract the jetlag that was sure to come. We had a busy schedule ahead of us, and trying to adjust to the time difference was not on the "to do" list. Neither was being in Rome without luggage, for that matter. The first order of business was to find at least a basic change of clothes.

Oh, by the way, every Italian I saw was about half my size. Trying to find pants tailored to a body shape and of a fashion that were anything like my own proved to be problematic. But we would survive. After all, the coffee was promising, and everywhere we looked a beautiful church with an amazing story awaited our exploration. With map in hand, we set out for what would be truly a remarkable week.

One night we were walking past a church and decided to slip in for a brief moment of prayer. My wife became focused on a cross in a way that I can only describe as Ignatian. While she was deep in prayer, a woman approached her and asked, "Excuse me, are you Mrs. Padgett?"

Linda was startled. She said yes, she was Mrs. Padgett, only to find out that the woman had attended some of the conferences I had done in the United States. We all gathered outside the church and agreed to meet again. The next few days were wonderful, as we became acquainted with more people in the Eternal City. It was as if we were meant by God to reach into one another's lives and celebrate the unity we had in Christ.

We visited the Sistine Chapel, which is smaller than you might imagine but more beautiful than one can articulate. For me one of the most powerful scenes depicted on the ceiling is that of God reaching out toward Adam. I found this to be such a witness of the human condition: Here the Creator of all is reaching, straining even, to touch humanity, and Adam can barely lift his arm, as if the interest of God were something to be considered but only when time permitted. I was certain that picture could be CliffsNotes of my life and of the rest of humanity as well. Well, maybe not everyone.

The only person in history who perfectly responded to God's reach was Mary. From infancy, and we could even say from conception, throughout her entire earthly life, the Virgin Mary was continually responding to the touch of God. It reminds me of 1 John 4:19: "We love, because he first loved us." Mary always noticed God reaching out to her, and her response was a continual straining and reaching back to him. It is a beautiful relief to know that at least once, God's creation reached back!

This should motivate us! Really, our journey in life will always have unexpected setbacks. We will certainly lose our luggage, encounter communication barriers, run out of funds (that is a different story), lose our way, and encounter bumps and detours along the path, but we will also happen upon new places, run into strangers who become lasting friends, and see beauty where we least imagined it. It is also true that we will not see how often God reaches toward us, but we can heighten our awareness and begin practicing this Marian way of reaching back to him. We need to remember that Mary is with us, trying to remind us of all that God has done and inviting us to reach back.

Today, simply stop a moment and try to see at least one way in which God is reaching out to you. Then see if you can reach back to him. Ask Our Lady to help you.

. . .

CHAPTER SIX

The Ecumenical Mary

Truth can never be compromised in our pursuit of ecumenism. This is true for both sides in any discussion on theology.

I am well aware of the heated dialogue between various denominations as well as the "ecumenical" confabulations people construct to avoid theological obstacles to unity. I've heard frustration on both sides of the fence as doctrines were dulled in order to aid agreement. Certainly there are many things with which we can and must be flexible, but truth is not duplicitous. The truth sets us free (see John 8:32).

Yet many have seen truth conveyed without love and so want to avoid conflict at all cost. Truth without love gains nothing (see 1 Corinthians 13:1–3). Love softens dialogue so as to appeal instead of repel. The truth spoken in love gives the listener a chance to make a free choice in a particular area.

Christians readily acknowledge that the Incarnation, the Redemption, and the Resurrection are the key points of the gospel; they *are*, in fact, the gospel. "For in Christ all the fullness of the Deity lives in bodily form, and you have been given fullness in Christ, who is the head over every power and authority" (Colossians 2:9–10, NIV). Many of my Protestant friends will shout to all that their inclusion in Christ has changed them dramatically. Many who hear this are motivated and touched. But mention Mary and her association with Christ in this Good News, and paralysis or fear overtakes the moment.

Yet Mary is not peripheral to the Christian faith. She is neither a trailer nor an introduction to the main feature. In fact, from the very beginning she is caught up by the director's choice in the main plot of this, the greatest of all stories. She is the queen of the valiant King. She is the heroine working with the hero in defeating the foe.

And what is the role given to this woman? She is invited into the mystery of the Incarnation as Mother. From this flows everything we will speak of concerning her. For the Incarnation's primary purpose is to show the beauty and greatness of God by redeeming those lost in sin and death. Mary and her seed crush the head of the Serpent with his offspring (see Genesis 3:15).

So let's look at some of the objections our Protestant brothers and sisters raise to the honor Catholics accord Mary. Let's seek the truth so that we can speak it in love.

Scriptural Dilemmas

Historically there have been certain verses in Scripture that seem problematic in the pursuit of Marian ecumenism. I mentioned one dilemma in chapter four, the issue of Jesus' "brethren" or brothers, which I hope I untangled for you. Here's another one.

There are times when Jesus appears to have a different under-standing of Mary's role in salvation than the Catholic Church does. How do Catholics rectify this apparent discrepancy?

In the Gospel of Luke we see one such instance of biblical dif-ficulty. At the arrival of his family, Jesus said to the crowd, "My mother and my brethren are those who hear the word of God and do it" (Luke 8:21). This statement seems to justify a lack of favor and a sense of indifference toward the Mother of God.

Another passage that seems to minimize the role of Mary is Luke 11:27–28: "A woman in the crowd raised her voice and said to him, 'Blessed is the womb that bore you, and the breasts that you sucked.' But he said, 'Blessed rather are those who hear the word of God and keep it!'"

For many Protestants little more needs to be said concerning Mary. In their opinion Catholics deny Scripture in giving the Blessed Mother undue honor and veneration. The line between orthodoxy and idolatry seems to blur, with Catholics on the lat-ter side.

And there is more scriptural evidence Protestants use to make their case. There is the twelve-year-old Jesus' peculiar comment to Joseph and Mary after they found him in the temple, "How is it that you sought me? Did you not know that I must be in my Father's house?" (Luke 2:49). And at the wedding at Cana, Jesus said to his mother, "O woman, what have you to do with me? My hour has not yet come" (John 2:49).

These passages seem to offer a different picture of Mary than the Catholic Church presents. Certainly she was honored to be the mother of Jesus, and for that she is uniquely special. But how can we pretend that she is to be heralded more than others when we see these references to her apparent misunderstandings of the mission of her son, juxtaposed with Christ's emphasis on being a doer of the Word over birthing the Word made flesh?

Blessed Among Women

I want to note two primary points in resolving the dilemma. The first point is that Jesus is God. This may seem obvious, but it is important to remember this within the context of the Scriptures.

The Word made flesh (John 1:14)—all deity in bodily form, the radiance of God's glory, and the exact representation of his nature (Hebrews 1:3)—would be sure to observe at all times the commandment "Honor your father and your mother, that your days may be long in the land which the LORD your God gives you" (Exodus 20:12). To disrespect one's parents had grave consequences: "'Cursed be he who dishonors his father or his mother.' And all the people shall say, 'Amen'" (Deuteronomy 27:16).

Jesus would have obeyed the fourth commandment better than did any other child. We all can agree to that. He was the model Hebrew son. And Mary was the proverbial virtuous woman, whose children "rise up and call her blessed" (Proverbs 31:28).

The second point is that Mary is the supreme example of "those who hear the word of God and do it." Therefore she fully is a part of Christ's higher understanding of family. Let's look at Luke 8:21 again, as well as its very important context.

We note that Jesus' mother and brothers wanted to see him (see Luke 8:20), but he seemed to be indifferent to their presence. Note that immediately previous to this event, Jesus had spoken this parable to the crowd:

> A sower went out to sow his seed; and as he sowed, some
> fell along the path, and was trodden under foot, and the
> birds of the air devoured it. And some fell on the rock; and
> as it grew up, it withered away, because it had no moisture.
> And some fell among thorns; and the thorns grew with it
> and choked it. And some fell into good soil and grew, and
> yielded a hundredfold.... He who has ears to hear, let him
> hear. (Luke 8:5–9)

It is within this context that we hear Jesus declare that his mother
and brothers are ones who hear God's word and do it. They are
"the good soil." They are those who, "hearing the word, hold it
fast in an honest and good heart, and bring forth fruit with
patience" (Luke 8:15).

At the same time people are beginning to see from Jesus' miracles and hear from his message that he is not like anyone else
they have met. He is the King of a kingdom into which all are
being invited. St. John the Baptist's servants have inquired as to
whether Jesus is the expected one, and Jesus has said, "Go and tell
John what you have seen and heard" (Luke 7:22).

Fr. M.J. Sheeben writes:

> Christ intended to show quite definitely that he stood
> toward Mary not in the same relation as an ordinary man
> to his mother; and He wished this shown not for her sake
> but for the sake of mankind. By making His own divine
> dignity felt, He pointed at the same time to the true form
> and meaning of Mary's motherhood as a divine motherhood.[1]

Mary *is* the fertile soil in which the seed was planted! She is the reflection of this image! She is the one who believed the word of God! Because of her belief, Jesus stands before the crowd! So the passage points the reader to the understanding of Jesus as the Word Incarnate. This mother of the Word made flesh is above all the example of how we, too, can say yes with our lives and become a doer of the Word and not a hearer only.

What about the wedding feast of Cana and the manner in which Jesus addressed Mary there? Isn't "woman" a derogatory way to refer to one's mother? Fr. Sheeben offers this insight:

> The address merely implies that Christ did not speak as a child, placed under Mary's maternal care and authority as at Nazareth, but in the exercise of his divine dignity and mission. The Hebrew expression (corresponding to "What is it to me and to thee, woman?"), intended not so much for Mary herself as for the bystanders, means simply that Christ, with regard to his mission, is withdrawn from the law of filial obedience: more correctly, that He will not comply with the request of Mary as Son of man, who depends on her, but as a more exalted son, the Son of God. For the words do not exclude the favorable response, but include it. . . .
>
> . . . He preferred to discourage an all too human and carnal idea of the relationship of his mother to himself, for this idea was linked up with a defective and an entirely false understanding of His higher, divine nature. . . .
>
> . . . Mary could become Mother of Christ, not as other mothers through the will of a man, but only through obe-

dience to the heavenly Father; her whole maternal relationship to Christ bears the characteristic of perfect surrender to the Father.[2]

Mary did not become Mother as do all other mothers. She became Mother because of her surrendered and freely given yes. She heard the word of God and embraced it within the fertile ground of her heart. She exemplified what Jesus wanted these followers to become. All they could see was the temporal and earthy understanding of family; Jesus wanted them to see the bigger picture of inclusion in the family of God, which happens with one's submission to the Word of God.

This is applicable to the message expressed in the phrase "Our Lady of All Nations, who once was Mary." Yes, we certainly see and understand her maternal role toward Jesus in time. But she was with him at Calvary and is the mother of all peoples now too. Don't see her only in terms of her blood ties with Jesus, for these are not the greatest aspect of her love for God. See the reality of how this all began: Mary said yes to God.

Too often Protestants emphasize Our Lady's being just like us. She is the best of us. She is the most faithful, most submissive, most devoted, and truly greatest lover and follower of Jesus. She is the one with whom God chose to identify most intimately. She is the fertile soil, saying yes to the will of the Father. She is the faithful follower of Jesus, constantly wanting others to embrace whatever her son says.

Finding the Way to Unity

How much service will we do Christian unity if we ignore the Marian truths of our faith? None. For by Mary Christ entered this world. She is the *Theotokos*, the Mother of God. She heralds for us all an intentional, intimate relation with the Trinity.

To eliminate Mary from ecumenical dialogue is to neuter the participation we have as God's creation in Christ's death and resurrection. If we say she isn't the recipient of the means to fulfill her role in the gospel, that she is somehow not unique in the opportunity of glorifying the Father, then what hope have we, those who were aliens and strangers because of sin (see 1 Peter 2:11)? If we have been brought near to God and are called to live in a manner that causes others to glorify God (1 Peter 2:12), then how can we imagine the Blessed Mother living in anything less than complete abandonment to the Father's will and total adoration of her child?

Mary is imperative to ecumenism because she is central to the story. We cannot expect participation in Christ's passion if we deny the very one who provides the body in the Incarnation. She is not simply the means for the end: She is not the mother of just the man. She is the Mother of God Incarnate.

Who among us would reject the opportunity to spend a day with any of the apostles, just for the sake of listening to one who touched, saw, and heard this One we love so much (see 1 John 1:1)? Yet think of a day spent with the very one whom he called Mother. Ponder what insight she would bring to your faith. Think of how he probably looked and sounded like her. What would we be like just after one day of listening to her tell us about Calvary?

So in our presentation of the Good News that has transformed us, how can we shy away from mentioning the very Mother of

God? Is this a ploy of the Serpent, still hissing his animosity toward this woman who crushed his head? I certainly think it is possible, plausible, and probable. (See chapter eleven for more on spiritual warfare.)

Mary exclaims her gratitude at this generous gift of being chosen by God in her Magnificat. She knows it is he who has initiated her privilege, and we can agree with him by calling her blessed among women. It is not our job to look at others and say they are not fit to be given such extravagant opportunities in glorifying Christ. We are not to compare ourselves; rather we are to rejoice in the success of others, to be in solidarity with those around us. This distinguishes us from the jealousy and envy of the world.

Let us not belittle the favor granted to Mary. God does not treat everyone exactly the same. Yet we all have the chance to fully follow Christ, to be the saints we were created to be. We are all invited into God's story. Many will call us crazy, delusional, misguided, or fixed upon an ancient fable; others will see the changes in us and believe.

Distinctions and differences among the saints exemplify the diversity within God.

> O LORD, how manifold are your works!
>> In wisdom you have made them all;
>> The earth is full of your creatures. (Psalm 104:24)

We should rejoice in Mary's saying yes, celebrate her faithfulness, and unite with her sufferings as she stands with Jesus at Calvary, where we see her united to the one purpose of Jesus, which is to glorify the Father in redeeming the lost.

It is important to remember that Mary desires ecumenism even more than we do. She wants all to come into the one fold, for she is devoted to the will of the Father in union with her Son, who prayed "that they may all be one,...so that the world may believe that God has sent the Son"(John 17:21). This is our prayer too.

Let us gratefully recall Mary's role in our spiritual birth. God comes to us through Mary; let us come to him through her. We do not diminish Christ's mediation in this way; rather we see its greater reach. He has included her in the heart of the Redemption; let us not exclude her in conveying its message. Jesus is intimately identified with his mother, so let us imitate our brother and be identified with her, too.

How can we be flexible in ecumenism? We can't be flexible at the expense of truth. We can in love, though, show others a picture of this woman, so embraced in Trinitarian love that her entire existence was a participation in glorifying God.

May our entire existence, too, glorify God the Father. St. Paul said it well:

> I always thank God for you because of his grace given you in Christ Jesus. For in him you have been enriched in every way—in all your speaking and in all your knowledge—because our testimony about Christ was confirmed in you. Therefore you do not lack any spiritual gift as you eagerly wait for our Lord Jesus Christ to be revealed. He will keep you strong to the end, so that you will be blameless on the day of our Lord Jesus Christ. (1 Corinthians 1:4–8, *NIV*)

CHAPTER SEVEN

Saint for the Saints

I hope you're starting to realize that you can really live for Christ better by entrusting yourself to Mary as your spiritual mother. She wants to help you become God's saint.

As I've said, if you look at the lives of the saints, you can see that many of them had a strong devotion to Our Lady. St. Thérèse of Lisieux had a powerful encounter with Our Lady when she was young, resulting in her healing from a serious illness. St. Pio loved to pray the rosary; he did it almost continually. St. Maximilian Kolbe published a magazine called *Knight of the Immaculate*, the aim of which was to "illuminate the truth and show the true way to happiness."[1]

So in pursuing Marian devotion, we are imitating the saints who have gone before us. This does not mean that we ignore the uniqueness of our calling; rather it means that we soak in the multiple ways our God has touched humanity. This should be a great encouragement to us. Why? Because God is not locked into one way when it comes to a person becoming a saint.

Reading about those who have gone before us and who model heroic virtue can encourage us to step up to the plate and confidently take a swing at what life throws in our path. We are certainly not here by accident, and we are not haphazardly put together or randomly placed on earth to try and figure life out on our own. God wants the very best for us, and he proves this by the many ways he reaches into people's lives. These people are just like you and me. They weren't born saints; rather they became saints.

Let's get down to brass tacks. I'd like to offer some practical advice on how Marian devotion increases your sanctity.

Pointing the Way

Think about it, you have the very mother Jesus did while he walked this earth. You also have the one Lord that all the saints depended upon. You certainly have access to the grace you need to live in a heroic fashion.

Is life difficult for you at home? Ask Jesus to work through you. Let him guide you to ways that you can love your family.

Are you made fun of at school? Maybe Jesus wants to use you to love others, even those who hurt you.

Do you worry about things that you can't control? Offer your concerns to Jesus, and let him take the wheel. That is what the saints did. God is faithful; we need to allow him to show us that.

Don't be afraid to ask for advice. You have the family of God at your disposal Ask all of heaven to assist you throughout the day.

Possibly you realize by now that I am nothing incredible on my own. Maybe you feel that way too. I decided a while ago to start trying to depend more on the saints, but what does that actually mean in everyday life?

Since I don't have visions or dreams, and since I don't have locutions or miraculous events taking place wherever I turn, I decided my dependence upon the saints would have to be a real work of faith. So even though I don't have special charismatic favors in seeing the members of the Church Triumphant in their beatific splendor, I decided to live my life as if I did. It might sound crazy, but I began to picture Mary with me in the morning as I prayed for her blessing upon my life. I would imagine (and still do) her putting her loving hands upon my head and blessing me in preparation for my day.

At various times throughout the day, I think of the saints coming up and making the Sign of the Cross on my forehead. I have begun to establish a relationship with these heroes of our faith, and it has actually been quite meaningful. You can do that, too.

We sometimes forget that being in the family of God is an actual fact that we can rely upon. These are real people who love Jesus and cheer us on as we journey toward him. Depend upon them!

Finally, I want to remind you of some simple actions you can take that will really make a difference in your life. First, to be a saint you must "soak" in the sacraments, so that you can have genuine encounters with Jesus. You need him! Mary always leads us to her son. I am confident that each time we go to Mass or reconciliation, Mary is leading the way.

Why do I say that? Because Our Lady is concerned about us, and she has taken a maternal responsibility for our salvation.

However many times we pray, "Thy will be done," the Blessed Mother assists us in bringing this petition to fruition. She wants God's will done in our lives! She will help us discern our vocation.

Secondly, we want to use sacramentals, holy things that assist us in knowing Christ more (see *CCC*, #1668–1670). Wearing a scapular or miraculous medal, praying the rosary and novenas, blessing ourselves with holy water—all help remind us that we are not here on earth just to make money or have fun. We are ambassadors for the true King, and our life must witness to this fact. Being reminded of all that God has for us, and longs to do through us, will help to keep his will in front of our wants and desires. In fact, the more we conscientiously use these spiritual reminders of sanctity, the more our will becomes linked to his.

Your life should include works of mercy, such as offering water to the thirsty and food to the hungry and visiting people in prison or the hospital. For younger folks it also means speaking a word of encouragement to the least important in your social group, giving the larger dessert to your sibling, and simply saying yes to your parents when you want to say no. These are all ways you can begin the journey toward sanctity. (Picking up your room and studying for exams are important parts of your vocation, too.)

If you feel unable to succeed in the task at hand, cry out for the aid of your family in heaven. Know that Mary is with you the whole time, loving you even when you struggle and fail. That is the most beautiful truth: You are loved even when you make a mistake. In our day and age, we are expected to be the best. God's love extends to us even at our worst!

Great Expectations

You have great potential, my friends. You will certainly be remembered for something after your life is spent. Some will remember your laughter, your antics, your cynicism, or even your sarcasm. Others will speak about how you went to the soup kitchen every weekend or made cards for the elderly in the assisted living facilities. In other words, your life will touch people and remind them of something beautiful (or ugly).

We should consider the reality of our life and its witness. The impact we have on those around us is eternal. This truth makes it really imperative that we run toward Jesus with everything we've got!

What would unfold if we really treated each other with dignity and respect? What would happen in our lives if we considered seriously the direction in which our words and deeds were leading us?

You should have great expectations for your spiritual walk, because God has great expectations for you. The wonderful news is that he has offered you the ability to succeed in this holy endeavor. Knowing this will help you in your relationships with others.

Consider C.S. Lewis's insight on how we should view one another:

> ... The load, or weight, or burden of my neighbor's glory should be laid on my back, a load so heavy that only humility can carry it, and the backs of the proud will be broken. It is a serious thing to live in a society of possible gods and

goddesses, to remember that the dullest and most uninter-
esting person you can talk to may one day be a creature
which, if you saw it now, you would be strongly tempted to
worship, or else a horror and a corruption such as you now
meet, if at all, only in a nightmare. All day long we are, in
some degree, helping each other to one or the other of
these destinations. It is in the light of these overwhelming
possibilities, it is with the awe and the circumspection
proper to them, that we should conduct all our dealings
with one another, all friendships, all loves, all play, all poli-
tics. There are no *ordinary* people. You have never talked to
a mere mortal.... [I]t is immortals whom we joke with,
work with, marry, snub, and exploit—immortal horrors or
everlasting splendors.... Next to the Blessed Sacrament
itself, your neighbor is the holiest object presented to your
senses.[2]

The Blessed Mother is looking upon you with true dignity and
respect. She has great expectations for you because of God's specific intentions concerning your existence. You are here for a reason, and your life testifies to more than you have imagined. Don't
be afraid to offer yourself completely to God.

Mary is our model and the witness of what can happen to a
heart entirely given over to Jesus. "Blessed is she who believed
that there would be a fulfillment of what was spoken to her from
the Lord" (Luke 1:45).

CHAPTER EIGHT

The Rosary: An Introduction

I want to take a look at the rosary. Don't panic; I am not going to give you a history or an analysis of its development. But I do think some reflection on it will show you that here is a useful tool for growing in holiness.

Blessed Pope John Paul II described the rosary as a "Christocentric prayer."[1] Sure, we say fifty Hail Marys each time we say the rosary, but the meditative focus is really on the mysteries, which take us through the life of Christ. We ask Mary to lead us to see Jesus more clearly in every moment of these Gospel reflections.

The rosary is packed full of insights on the life of Jesus, many of which are applicable to our own joyful, luminous, sorrowful, and glorious moments. Mary is there to show us how to live, love, and listen to the Lord.

The Mysteries

The joyful mysteries come first. In the Annunciation, the Visitation, the Nativity, the Presentation, and the Finding of Jesus in the Temple, we watch Mary willingly give herself over to God's love and bring Jesus to others. We rejoice with her at the favors she receives from heaven.

Mary brings the Child to the world, even while he is within her womb. She comes to Elizabeth, who with her son is filled with God's Spirit. After the Lord's birth Mary shows him to the shepherds and to the kings from afar. She brings Jesus to Simeon and the prophetess Anna, and their lives are complete with having looked upon the Anointed One (see Matthew 2:1–12; Luke 1:39–56; 2:8–18, 25–38). Mary rejoices in the mission of her son from the start.

The luminous mysteries, the mysteries of light, focus on Christ's ministry, beginning with his baptism by John in the Jordan, the wedding feast at Cana, and the proclamation of the kingdom of God, which of course Mary was committed to from the first moment of her existence. She rejoices in the Transfiguration of Our Lord, for here the disciples realize that he is not another teacher among many but in fact the Anointed of God, the Christ. Mary, too, knows the depth of the encounter with Christ that the disciples receive in the Eucharist, which is similar to her intimate experience with him at the Incarnation.

In contemplating the sorrowful mysteries, we recognize that every life—even that of Jesus, the perfect man—has moments of struggle and frustration. Mary, too, has experienced sorrow. She is preserved from sin yet willingly suffers for our salvation. She unites herself to the mission of her son, which is our redemption.

At the agony in the garden, we see the disciples fall asleep and then run from the cross, but Mary goes to Golgotha. She allows her heart to be pierced by the sword of suffering on our behalf as Jesus is scourged and crowned with thorns. Jesus walks to Calvary with a great weight, and Mary, too, journeys toward this crucifixion. We can stand with her beneath Jesus at Calvary.

Then come the glorious mysteries. Jesus is resurrected from the dead, and all rejoice! The joy of the disciples must have paled in comparison to the celebration and excitement of Our Lady. She knew what Jesus' resurrection meant. It was more than simply the return of a son or an old friend; it was victory over sin and death for all!

Mary watched Jesus ascend into heaven and felt the familiar presence of the Spirit as he fell upon the Church at Pentecost. She was assumed into heaven to spend forever with her son and reign as our queen. We can see the culmination of Christ's salvific mission and the role Our Lady has been granted in it. It is glorious indeed.

Rosary Quotes

Many saints loved and promoted the rosary. Here are quotes from some about this wonderful way to sanctity:

> By the Rosary the darkness of heresy has been dispelled, and the light of the Catholic Faith shines out in all its brilliancy. [2]

> —Pope St. Pius V

... Urban IV, testified that "every day the Rosary obtained fresh boon for Christianity." Sixtus IV declared that this method of prayer "redounded to the honor of God and the Blessed Virgin, and was well suited to obviate impending dangers"; Leo X that "it was instituted to oppose pernicious heresiarchs and heresies"; while Julius III called it "the glory of the Church." So also St. Pius V, that "with the spread of this devotion the meditations of the faithful have begun to be more inflamed, their prayers more fervent...."[3]

—Pope Leo XIII

To the honor of Mary, the great Mother of God, for a perpetual remembrance of the prayer for her protection offered among all nations throughout the month of October to her Most Pure Heart; as an enduring testimony of the unbounded trust which we put in our most loving Mother, and in order that we may day by day more and more obtain her favorable aid: we will and decree that in the Litany of Loreto, after the invocation, "Queen conceived without original sin," shall be added the suffrage, "Queen of the most Holy Rosary, pray for us." [4]

—Pope Leo XIII

In the Rosary, along with the most beautiful and efficacious prayers arranged in an orderly pattern, the chief mysteries of our religion follow one another, brought before our mind for contemplation: first of all the mysteries in which the Word was made flesh in Mary, the inviolate Virgin and Mother, performs her maternal duties for him with a holy joy; there come then the sorrows, the agony and death of the suffering Christ, the price at which the salvation of our race was accomplished; then follow the mysteries full of his glory, his triumph over death, the Ascension into heaven, the sending of the Holy Spirit, the resplendent brightness of Mary received among the stars, and finally the everlasting glory of all the Saints in heaven united with the glory of the Mother and her Son.[5]

—Pope Leo XIII

If you say the Rosary faithfully until death, I do assure you that, in spite of the gravity of your sins "you shall receive a never-fading crown of glory." Even if you are on the brink of damnation, even if you have one foot in hell, even if you have sold your soul to the devil as sorcerers do who practice black magic, and even if you are a heretic as obstinate as a devil, sooner or later you will be converted and will amend your life and will save your soul, if—and mark well what I say—if you say the Holy Rosary devoutly every day until death for the purpose of knowing the truth and obtaining contrition and pardon for your sins.[6]

—St. Louis de Montfort

CHAPTER NINE

The Rosary, Family Style

Praying the rosary as a family can be a participation in the passion of Christ. If you are a parent, you will certainly agree that family prayers of any kind can be a form of redemptive suffering unlike any other. We could easily ask ourselves, why even start a tradition of prayer that will only end in frustration? Why place ourselves upon this path of agony?

I think deep down inside we know that this suffering has life-giving repercussions. In fact, I am confident that you will find a wonderful beauty alongside the challenging madness of gathered intercession. So let us look at the parental call to prayer and its benefits, particularly its culmination in our resurrection with Christ.

The Call

If you are not already praying as a family, the first step is the call. Just trying to gather the children for evening rosary can be a feat in itself. In fact, I dare say the parting of the Red Sea is seen by many families as a small act of divine intervention compared to finding their kids and gathering them into one location for a bit of prayer.

Families are busy these days. For many homes it is rare to have everyone gathered together for supper, let alone an established prayer experience. Add to that the nomadic tendencies of little ones, and we have a real struggle on our hands.

Through television and computers our kids are constantly entertained. The rosary does not offer many moments of personal feel-good gratification, nor the glam and glitz of modern technology, so it can seem almost pointless in the spiritual development of our young people. Isn't there something better to do with our time? Isn't there a stronger way to invite our children into prayer, one that is "fun"?

Yet we know that the family rosary has beautiful ramifications in terms of spiritual growth. Although we may not "feel" our children being touched during this time—in fact, it may seem that they are far from interested in what we're doing—the truth is that the repetition of the prayers and the meditations upon the mysteries of the rosary can exert tremendous power to form them in God's image.

A positive step forward could be simply picking two nights a week to start this adventure in prayer. It is important to make the call heard throughout your home. Prayer time must be as important to you as your child's sporting events.

For families with young children, the struggle in gathering them together can seem endless. I understand this very well, being the father of eight. But think about the energy we extend to collect the children for school, doctor appointments, or even a trip to the zoo.

Our spiritual health has far greater implications than any physical health concerns or academic achievements ever will.

Let me simply state that the rosary is not the latest expression of "fun," nor is it an ancient prayer needing a technological boost to lure the masses into its beauty. Rather the rosary is an opportunity for us to settle into the rhythm of God's life through the Person of Jesus Christ. As we see joyful, luminous, sorrowful, and even glorious events unfold before us daily, we can unite our experiences with those of the Holy Family.

Suffering and the Cross

Parents may feel that the rosary is a time of purgation. With children weeping and gnashing their teeth, this prayer time, instead of being a heavenly experience, seems to reflect a place of pain and suffering. I can certainly understand that. The rosary is a chance for us to practice self-donation in more ways than one.

In our home, as we gather for evening rosary, exhaustion seems to overwhelm me. The moment I sit down, I feel, unfortunately, very much like the disciples who fell asleep in the garden during Jesus' agony. There have been times when I have actually drifted off in the middle of a Hail Mary, only to be startled awake by hearing my family pray a little louder, inviting me back to the land of the living.

It isn't just a personal struggle though. During the rosary children will occasionally become distracted. (What I really want to say is that they will occasionally be engaged in the prayer.) It seems that all of the Hail Marys become a bit too much for little ones who have been nursed on the electronic pabulum of our age.

Many evenings my little ones gather in the living room with rosaries in hand not for the purpose of participating in the prayers but with intentions of inflicting torture on their siblings. The preferred use of the beads is to whip their brothers and sisters into shape. Those in a more peaceful mood might make their rosaries into what could possibly be marketed as a new workout tool. They put their feet in the circle of the beads, pull on the crucifix, and stretch.

In our home we invite the little ones to look at books with pictures of the mysteries, yet it is inevitable that one particular book becomes the one that every child must hold in his or her lap. It becomes a struggle to continue in prayer with the little ones arguing—and the phone ringing, the homework looming, the babies crying, the teenagers mumbling, food digesting, exhaustion overwhelming. And all the while we wonder, will any of this really make a difference? Is there a light at the end of the tunnel?

The Resurrection

Hope can come with astonishing clarity, like a small ray of sunshine within the storm. One day—Good Friday, in fact—my four-year-old son led the fourth sorrowful mystery in our family for the first time. We all clapped as he finished it. Everyone in the family was so proud and excited at this beautiful moment. This glorious opportunity would not have been mine if we were not persistent in praying the family rosary.

I do understand the exhaustion and sibling struggles. I can relate with the pull in many different directions. However, in the end, teaching our children to focus on the beauty of God's love within time and on his invitation to spend eternity with him is the catechesis we as parents are asked to convey. God gave me these children in order to bring them to heaven.

In today's society we applaud those who have great fame and success. Our children are trained by the world to embrace those who are popular, athletic, and financially successful. As Catholic parents we are to instill in our children the futility of worldly attachment and approval, in order that they might pursue the pearl of great price. We are to lead our children to the beauty of Christ Jesus, imploring them to seek God above all else.

Entrusting our families to the maternity of the Blessed Mother Mary enables us to achieve our goal as parents. She is willing and able to instruct us as we train our children in the way they should go. One sure way of getting in step with our mother's teaching is to meditate upon the mysteries of the rosary. Leading our family into this meditation is not easy, nor is it always contemplative or the conduit for warm and fuzzy feelings. The importance and value of the rosary is there nonetheless.

Patiently finding new ways to bring out the mysteries—through Scripture reading, looking at photos, or asking for reflections after each decade—can engage us and our children in these moments of prayer. Make the call heard in your family, invite them into the rhythm of life by meditating upon the beauty of God in time, and take all of the struggles of this rosary time and place them upon the cross, realizing that the impact you are making in your children's lives is leading them to the beauty of the Resurrection.

Practical Family Prayer

Given the value of family prayer, I want to offer a variety of ideas to help engage children in it and help your whole family approach it with a sense of expectancy. This is not a success story on my part; rather it is advice and insight that I, too, am trying to implement daily within our home. The success will be found at the finish line, not during the race itself.

Consistency

We must begin with a consistent prayer time. There are some families that struggle, due to the crazy schedules of life, to even have regularity in dining experiences, but having a consistent time for prayer will help establish the rhythm your family needs. Even if it has been a busy day and there is still lots of homework to complete, our children know that rosary time is not something that can be ignored. Every night we try and pray five decades of the rosary. Over time the older ones have come to accept this, and the younger ones don't know of anything different.

The Place

In the room where we pray, there are pictures of Mary and Jesus, along with statues of St. Jude and St. Joseph, the Pieta, and even some relics of our favorite saints. My goal for this place of prayer is that, even if the children are not consciously engaged in the rosary that night, all that is around them invites them into the family of God.

The Church has long used stained glass windows as catechetical devices for young children and the illiterate. Our family uses biblical images and Catholic reminders to the same end.

Responsibilities

The designation of responsibilities helps make our family prayer a bit more peaceful—well, somewhat anyway. The older ones in our home have the responsibility of changing diapers and putting pajamas on the smaller ones. Meanwhile someone is designated to clear off the dinner table.

A couple of the younger kids usually begin to argue about who will bring out the rosaries for prayer. Sometimes it will be three kids at once running into the back room, climbing over one another and creating a great amount of chaos in what one would hope could be a preparation for peace. Seeing tempers flare over who will bring out the rosaries might tempt one to think prayer useless in family life. Be encouraged though, because such frustration is common to most families, and I am sure it is one of the ploys of the enemy to get families to give up on prayer.

In the end it is usually the child who exemplifies the greatest calm who gets the privilege of passing out the beads. Once the beads are distributed, expect a new commotion to break out at the other side of the room, as the desire to light the candle unfolds into accusations of insensitivities and great injustices.

With the number of kids we have, there is always one crying, sleeping, bleeding, or burping by the time the rosary begins, ensuring that our night remains interesting. Knowing this turmoil will take place, we can avoid a few problems by designating responsibilities ahead of time. But certainly not all storms will be calmed to everyone's satisfaction, and that is OK.

Good Intentions

There are two points I wish to make concerning good intentions.

First, most parents who want to pray the rosary with their family should know from the start that this is a noble and beautiful service to their homes and to the Church as a whole. It isn't an easy task, but certainly these good intentions do not go unnoticed by our loving God.

My second point is a play on the word *intention*. Praying the rosary for some specific intention helps to make this event one that has purpose for all. In our family we go around the room and ask what we should pray for, and from young to old, there is always something or someone to include. We have heard the call for intercession for those who are having children, for an end to abortion, and even for divine assistance for "cool guy," my son's imaginary friend. We might offer the whole rosary for those for whom nobody is praying.

Engaging the Senses

It is widely proven that individuals learn in very unique and specific ways. Some are tactile and hands-on, while other people can simply read from a book and everything makes complete sense to them. Prayer is a very personal experience. This habit of dialogue with God will be more meaningful if the child is able to approach it from his or her area of comfort.

Certainly this exploration in prayer has to fit within the rhythm of the family setting. Let's press this out a bit more for practicality.

Allowing a child to pick from the pile of rosaries is an excellent practice. The color and size of the beads engage their senses of sight and touch. (For my little children it also impacts their sense of taste, as at least one is bound to try eating the rosary before we've finished the Apostles' Creed.)

As I mentioned before, many times we allow our younger children to hold and look at books that depict the mysteries through paintings, drawings, and photos. We have also purchased picture cards for each mystery of the rosary and laminated them so they can be passed around and endure the experience. These pictures enable the children to "see" what we are praying about.

We have learned to be creative in order to get the kids involved in the actual prayer. Usually one child will lead a mystery, and I might ask before or after that mystery why the child chose to pray that one. I sometimes ask the children what stood out for them during a particular mystery or what new thought occurred to them that night. Sometimes my wife and I describe a mystery from a deeper perspective. Occasionally we read a Scripture passage or ask a question to draw everyone into the mystery.

Then again, there are nights when we were ready for the kids to be in bed hours before, so we just modify our prayer time. You know your family, so apply these suggestions to your needs.

Discipline

Let's be honest here. Even if we have settled into a room filled with reminders of our faith, passed out rosaries and picture books, lit candles, offered intentions for the upcoming prayer, and interjected small reflections and discussion during the decades, before we know it an avalanche of chaos can break loose. The truth is that this happens far more often than does the enveloping peace that we as parents are waiting for. Why does this chaos happen?

For starters, if this is a new practice in your home, then give yourself a break. It takes years to establish habits and rhythms in your family life, so it will likely take more than a few weeks for this practice of prayer to become the norm.

We also have to remember that family prayer is a supernatural force that the enemy would like to stop at all costs. Not only will the family who pray together stay together, but they will impact all of eternity together. Your intercession may make all the difference in a person's recovery to health, conversion to Christ, or endurance in difficult times. Your family prayers may in fact deliver countless souls from purgatory.

Being disciplined in prayer does not mean that warm and fuzzy feelings will accompany every decade. In fact, expect the dark night of the soul in rosary time. But also realize that your persistence in prayer, without emotion and consolation, will be maturity exemplified to all involved. And the ramifications of disciplined prayer and intercession are eternal!

There is another aspect of discipline that you may need to apply. That is, there may be moments when children are completely out of sync with the happenings of the evening. Here are some practical considerations for such breakdowns.

If you find that one child is choking another with a rosary, it is time to take the rosary away, as well as the offender. In our home we have a crib set up in another room called the "happy bed." This is reserved for times when a little one goes a bit bonkers. There he or she can regroup and become "happy" without disrupting the whole family.

There are occasions when the little ones are so crazy with exhaustion or sugar that we put them in bed a little early. Sometimes the threat of being placed in bed is enough to sober them up. After all, praying the rosary is certainly preferable to going to bed early.

Your family is unique, and I don't know what will work for you. But I am sure the Lord will give you graces to succeed in this area. He wants our families to be given over to him in prayer. And certainly Our Lady will teach us how this can work in our home.

What We Want

We need to realize that it is OK to experiment with all of these areas: books, candles, pictures, and so on. If you have a struggle in one room, try praying somewhere else till you find a place that works well. Maybe your kids are more settled right before bedtime instead of right after dinner. Pray at a time that works best for you.

The first time I experienced a family rosary was as a guest in the home of a large family. Parents and children gathered in one bedroom for evening prayer. There were multiple bunk beds and chairs, with pillows and blankets all over the floor. The lights were turned off. Within moments of the rosary's beginning, the little kids were sleeping.

I was blown away by the experience. If I were to do prayer in my home exactly as that family did, I would be out cold right after the first Our Father. The lights need to be on, or I am off to la-la land. This points again to the fact that every family needs to adjust the discipline of family prayer in a way that works for them.

In conclusion I will simply say that if we want a family rosary, then it will become a part of our life. Look at it like this: If our kids want to be in sports, they try out and do whatever it takes to get to practices and games. If we want to go to a movie, have a certain food for dinner, or have a little time to ourselves, then we do what it takes to make these wants reality. If we want to make the family rosary more than an idea, it's going to take lots of work, but it will become more natural the more we work at it.

Countless saints attest to the amazing fruit of this prayer. Some seemed to pray it constantly. Others found the rosary difficult to pray. So if you find the family rosary a battle of some sort, realize that you are not alone in this heroic effort to raise your children in the presence of Christ.

I have in my mind the ideal rosary night with my family, but honestly, it is rare that that ideal becomes reality. What are so beautiful though are the surprises of the family rosary: children helping their siblings find the mystery in a picture book, one who has seemed completely indifferent the last two years leading a decade, another beginning to move through the beads along with the prayers. You will notice these moments of victory along the way, too.

Please don't give up. You may not realize the ramifications of what you are doing, but the consequences of your actions are eternal. Hang in there, and know that Mary is ready to shower your family with the beauty of her son.

. . .

CHAPTER TEN

Mary at Mass

God gives us opportunities every day to be like Mary. One of the greatest is the Mass, where we offer ourselves with and in Christ back to the Father in the love of the Holy Spirit.

Vatican II called the faithful to "full, conscious, and active participation" in the one sacrifice at the Mass.[1] Whether in silence or in spoken words, we offer ourselves through the priest to the Father. We are the small and insignificant gifts of bread and wine, to be "blessed," "broken," and "given" by the hands of Jesus. We join the priest in prayer as we present to the Father, through the Holy Spirit, the Son who is now sacramentally present upon the altar.

The redemption of humankind was a one-time event with everlasting consequences. For Catholics the Holy Sacrifice of the Mass is a re-presenting of that redemption at Calvary, and because of this it is important for us to fully enter into it. Jesus "took bread, and when he had given thanks he broke it and gave it to them, saying, 'This is my body which is given for you. Do this in remembrance of me'" (Luke 22:19).

The Cross

Jesus—body, blood, soul, and divinity—paid the debt for our sins by offering himself as an unblemished sacrifice. This self-offering more than satisfied justice. We, as members of his body, are asked to participate in Christ's death by taking up our cross and being crucified with him, so that we will be resurrected with him as well (see Luke 9:23; Galatians 2:20; 6:14; Philippians 3:10–11). And so we cling to the cross and remind ourselves of its saving grace.

The fifteen prayers of St. Bridget invoke the Lord to remember his suffering as he hears our pleas for mercy. For example:

> O Jesus! Strong lion, immortal and invincible King,
> remember the pain Thou didst endure when all Thy
>   strength,
> both moral and physical, was entirely exhausted;
> Thou didst bow Thy Head, saying: "It is consummated."
>
> Through this anguish and grief,
> I beg of Thee, Lord Jesus,
> to have mercy on me at the hour of my death
> when my mind will be greatly troubled and my soul will be
>   in anguish. Amen.[2]

The sacrifice of Christ is the remedy for our sin. We need to be reminded of this regularly.

At Mass we are invited to offer back to the Father the reality of Jesus' sacrifice. Even before the Consecration we offer ourselves up along with the humble bread and wine.

It is the priest who makes Christ present through the action of the Holy Spirit; there is no way the laity could muster Christ's salvific presence. But once a priest has done so, we, too, can offer to the Father the real presence of Christ in the Eucharist. In fact, an angel who appeared to the children at Fatima instructed them to offer up the Body, Blood, soul, and divinity of our Eucharistic Lord in the tabernacles of the world for those still in need of salvation.[3]

It is Jesus alone in the Eucharist, because this Holy Sacrifice of the Mass is a re-presentation of Calvary, and certainly only Jesus died on the cross, *not* Jesus and bread or Jesus along with wine. Some people read the sixth chapter of the Gospel of St. John and assume that the Bread of Life is only symbolic, but this bespeaks a careless reading. Note, for instance, that some in the crowd walked away, and Jesus made no attempt to soften his words in order to keep them with him (see John 6:66).

Some Protestant ecclesiology (specifically, that which is not "high church") tries to imitate portions of the Last Supper as a commemorative event. Their celebration is a remembrance of the past with gratitude. It comes close to realizing that we are called to do and be like Jesus but stops short of believing in the literal presence of Jesus in the Eucharist.

The Catholic Mass, on the other hand, is the true reenactment of the Last Supper. The Church wants us to remember the moment of Christ's offering with affection, but it invites us to go further and enter into the very act of redemption at every Mass. This takes on a depth that most fundamentalist Protestant denominations honestly cannot comprehend.

When the priest stands at Mass and says, "This is my body," he is speaking as another Christ. When we say, "May the Lord accept the sacrifice at your hands," it is with the understanding that the priest is offering the once-and-for-all sacrificial offering as another Christ. It is a sharing in the one priesthood of Christ!

Now, this is a mystery, but we Catholics receive the Lord Jesus literally within ourselves. The Mass allows us to be entirely enveloped in the Passion.

The Church isn't a formulation of rules and practices but a family under authority. Catholics are not free to modify this representation. We do not flow with the trends or latest teaching techniques that "experts" insist will make our churches grow and become more relevant. The Mass was done right the first time! We embrace it in all its grandeur.

The Mass is all about the cross. Two thousand years ago on Calvary, Jesus Christ was nailed to the cross, and there he died for all of us. It is this Jesus Christ who comes to us in Communion.

Real Love

We are to be people of the Eucharist. When we enter a church and genuflect before entering a pew, we show reverence for the real presence of Christ in the Blessed Sacrament, residing in the tabernacle. When we come forward to receive Communion, we genuflect or bow in recognition of the fact that Jesus is truly before us and is entering into our lives in all his humility. We do not kneel before bread.

The real presence of Christ is no novel idea. Early Church leaders, some trained by the apostles of Christ, emphatically proclaimed the literal presence of Christ in the Eucharist. In fact, they recognized the need to become Eucharistic in their total identification with Christ. The Eucharist is an invitation for us, too, to enter into the reality of what Our Lord has done for us.

Inasmuch as we fully, actively, and consciously participate in the Mass, we in actuality love God. This love is not simply a notion or a cerebral ideology meant to entertain us; rather it is an active and fruitful love that impacts those around us. In other words, if you say that you love God, then you should enter into the greatest "loving" of humanity through the filial love of Christ extended to the Father at Mass.

What we have at Mass is an invitation to realize the beauty of the unseen. The Word became flesh and dwells among us, and through his *kenosis* we are redeemed and now invited into the love of the Trinity as children. The very Spirit of God within us cries out, "Abba!" "Father!" (Romans 8:15). Thus the Mass is heaven within time.

As we comprehend the finality of Jesus' self-donation to the Father in the Holy Spirit, we can become more generous in the priesthood of the believer. Each time the priest offers Jesus back to the Father, we, too, are invited to lift our hearts to the Lord in union with this perfect sacrifice. Our love and gift of self are small and inadequate, yet as members of the mystical body of Christ, we are identified with Jesus. He is the Head of the body, so we can receive the fullness of love extended to him.

So if you want to know what real love looks like, actively offer yourself along with Christ back to the Father in the love of the Holy Spirit at every Mass. If you want to love Jesus, enter into the

Mass with joyful reverence, seeing yourself now in Christ through baptism.

This love is not dependent upon our emotions. It would be impossible for our emotions to handle or, for that matter, even comprehend the fullness of this union. I find this so magnificent, that when we unite ourselves with Christ in the holy sacrifice of the Mass, we can truly love God in the most perfect way.

Is Mary at Mass?

Absolutely.

In the Penitential Rite we "ask blessed Mary, ever virgin," to pray for us. We bow our heads at the words of the Creed, "By the power of the Holy Spirit, he was born of the Virgin Mary and became man." We are ever cognizant of Mary's yes, for without the Incarnation there would be no Redemption.

The Eucharistic Prayer reminds us of Mary's living sacrifice, in union with her Son, in the love of her Spouse, the Holy Spirit, to the glory of God the Father. Mary willingly offers her only child back to the Father on our behalf, just as we are called to actively unite ourselves with the Son's gift to the Father. She models perfectly the priesthood of the believer: "Like living stones be yourselves built into a spiritual house, to be a holy priesthood, to offer spiritual sacrifices acceptable to God through Jesus Christ" (1 Peter 2:5).

At Mass we stand with the Sorrowful Mother at the foot of the cross, aching for the Redemption to unfold for souls trapped in sin and death. The more we follow Mary's witness at the cross, the more deeply we comprehend our own call to take up our cross and follow Christ.

Mary is especially a model for us in reverent reception of the Eucharist. She eagerly welcomed the Messiah in her womb with the words "Let it be to me according to your word" (Luke 1:38). Our prayer before Communion is "Lord, I am not worthy," and rightly so. We ask for the grace of which Mary was so full as we approach the altar and welcome the Lord into our bodies. We then carry him to others, as Mary brought him to the world.

Mary invites us to actively love Jesus more and more by participating in the greatest act of love—Jesus' sacrifice and gift to the Father in the love of the Holy Spirit at Calvary. This is the Mass.

. . .

CHAPTER ELEVEN

The Attack

We tend to forget that there is a war going on spiritually. Satan does not take the gospel lightly. When we receive and then try to convey its life-changing message, we shouldn't be surprised to see his opposition. The evil one has strategies for scrambling the meaning and the presentation of the message.

The Church has battled heresies and false teachers since her infancy. Even St. Paul battled the Judaizers, who were influencing the Church in Galatia. The Lord has preserved the integrity of the Church's doctrines through the Holy Spirit. With the teaching of the apostles on down to faithful scholars and holy saints, we have seen these heresies defeated.

I am not saying that we should look for a demon behind every bush or bramble; rather we must be cognizant of the real spiritual battles in which we are involved. And we needn't fear, for Jesus has promised us victory.

Mary is our advocate in the battle: She is a sure defense against the evil one and all his current lies, for she is the one who crushes the head of the Serpent. Her life was one of entire devotion to God, in union with her seed.

In the Middle Ages the Church had quite a task in battling the Albigensian teaching, which held that there were two equal and dueling gods: one good, the other evil. St. Dominic recommended praying 150 Hail Marys a day—a practice that heralded the rosary's development—which was easier for the laity to observe than the traditional monastic prayer of the same number of psalms. We are not surprised to see that this devoted follower of Our Lady soon began to see many convert to the faith and even more repent of their Albigensian beliefs.

In the present times of confusion and misunderstanding in the Church and in our world, we can breathe more easily knowing that Mary is our mother and that she is with us in the battle.

War on the Family

One of the greatest attacks Satan has schemed in our present day is against motherhood, fatherhood, and the family overall. Pope John Paul II wrote in *Familiaris Consortio*, his apostolic exhortation on the family:

> ... [T]he true advancement of women requires that clear recognition be given to the value of their maternal and family role, by comparison with all other public roles and all other professions. Furthermore, these roles and professions should be harmoniously combined, if we wish the evolution of society and culture to be truly and fully human....
>
> Furthermore, the mentality which honors women more for their work outside the home than for their work within

the family must be overcome. This requires that men should truly esteem and love women with total respect for their personal dignity, and that society should create and develop conditions favoring work in the home.[1]

Our society pushes the masculinization of women. To feel accepted in our generation, women must accomplish everything a man does but with greater success. Often they must deny things that reflect their natural femininity, the very reality of who they are.

Just look at what we see today. To be a "stay-at-home mom" is considered a second-rate job, which many insist causes the mind to go to pudding. A woman who has more than three children is considered a poster representative for welfare candidacy. Abortion has become "normal," residing under the banner of "choice." Motherhood is kept at bay, even to the point of murdering the child. The ideals of loving one's husband, sticking to him for life, raising a family, and pursuing God are, to many, vestiges from the days of *Little House on the Prairie,* and anything resembling a favorable nod toward that time is considered scandalous, threatening everything women have worked so hard to achieve.

Cardinal Joseph Ratzinger, now Pope Benedict XVI, was interviewed in the late eighties, and his words are still profound in their analysis of the societal distortion of the feminine: "… To respect biology is to respect God himself, hence to safeguard his creatures."

According to Ratzinger, this, too, is the fruit "of the opulent West and of its intellectual *establishment.*" Feminine radicalism "announces a liberation that is a salvation different from, if not opposed to, the Christian conception." But, he warns: "The men and above all the women who are experiencing the fruits of this presumed post-Christian salvation must realistically ask themselves if this really signifies an increase of happiness, a greater balance, a vital synthesis, richer than the one discarded because it was deemed to be obsolete."…

> …[I]t is precisely woman who is paying the greatest price. Motherhood and virginity (the two loftiest values in which she realizes her profoundest vocation) have become values that are in opposition to the dominant ones. Woman, who is creative in the truest sense of the word by giving life, does not "produce," however, in that technical sense which is the only one that is valued by a society more masculine than ever in its cult of efficiency. She is being convinced that the aim is to "liberate" her, "emancipate" her, by encouraging her to masculinize herself, thus bringing her into conformity with the culture of production and subjecting her to the control of the masculine society of technicians, of salesmen, of politicians who seek profit and power, organizing everything, marketing everything, instrumentalizing everything for their own ends. While asserting that sexual differentiation is in reality secondary (and, accordingly, denying the body itself as an incarnation of the spirit in a sexual being), woman is robbed not only of motherhood but also of the free choice of virginity. Yet, just as man cannot procreate without her, likewise he cannot be virgin save by "imitat-

ing" woman who, also in this way, has a surpassing value as "sign," as "example" for the other part of humanity.[2]

Has there been a need in our society to reconsider stereotypes, abolish sexual harassment, and confront belittling caricatures of women? Absolutely! But in striving for independence, many women have acquiesced to a teaching and a lifestyle that have demonic undertones.

The media and feminist pundits would try to convince us that the next generation doesn't need mothers. Two men can raise a child, the daycare can be responsible 90 percent of the time for little ones, and a surrogate can birth our baby. Fatherhood is also in shambles. If need be, medical science can get children started in a test tube. Women are forced to play both mom and dad due to the staggering divorce rates. And still people ask what planet we are from if we think two spouses committed for life are the best plan for a family.

War on Mary

I am sure that many people consider me an out-of-touch, old-fashioned, behind-the-times type of guy, but I ask you to hear me out. What if this confusion within the sexes comes down to an intentional scheme to distort humanity's understanding of the Trinity and the Blessed Mother? Doesn't belittling maternity also belittle the love of the Blessed Virgin Mary for all humanity? This is certainly the intention of the Serpent, who has always been trying to wound the heel of the one who has crushed his head with her Seed (see Genesis 3:15 again).

How many people consider devotion to the Blessed Mother odd? Those who see no need for a mother are not about to ask for one, even a divine one. In our hallucination, which we think is reality, we lash out at this mother who longs to comfort our fevered souls. She faithfully cares for us, praying and interceding, while we pretend she isn't there. We pull a teenage tantrum and storm out of the Blessed Mother's influential reach, pursuing whatever we can to fill the hole we have in our life, abandoning love once again.

In many ways the fear of being unloved is central to this deception. Society tells people that finding love in parents, marriage, and children, along with having a healthy appreciation for self, is a pie-in-the-sky notion that can only lead to heartbreak and bondage. What image of love are they left to pursue? An inadequate one.

Self-gratification is the dominant force. Acceptance at all cost and using others and self as means to an end destroy the conscience and deafen the ears to the still small voice of God, which calls our prodigal selves to come home. This heavenly home— where there is a Father, brother, mother, and Spirit of love—is the place of satisfaction and clarity.

I am certainly not saying that people who have to use daycare are submitting to the demonic. Nor are families in which a spouse has left or passed away, leaving one to be mother and father. I do not pretend that women are incapable of doing "a man's job"; actually, most of the women I know are more capable than I am in about anything I can think of. These are not jabs directed at individuals; rather this is a societal issue needing to be addressed.

We must look at the whole picture.

There is an undercurrent that wants to take you from the Blessed Mother's love. There is an enemy that hisses for your soul. He tries to convince you that Holy Mother Church is some ancient, uninterested, authoritarian, hierarchical force that isn't relevant in this age of intellectual sobriety. We must recognize this message for what it is: demonic.

I stand in opposition to such lies. I choose to become foolish in the world's eyes, in order that I might love Christ and his mother. I rest at peace in my mother's arms, as she continues to lead me closer to her son.

I am not a prophet or some half-crazed religious nut who has lost touch with reality. I am a man who has fallen in love with the One who loved me more than I could ever deserve. I have been changed from what was old and dying into a living creation, who can reflect love and thrive on it. I am able to look my wife in the eye and know that we are reflecting in two unique ways the reality of Christ's love, that we are a limited incarnation of the Trinity among many. We manifest aspects of God that reflect who we are in our differences and similarities.

We need to be satisfied in our diversity, to recognize Divine Providence at work. We are then free to come to a deeper understanding of who we are and who we are called to be. We are free to be mothered again. And in the beauty of maternity, we can grow in living entirely for God and for one another.

Mary is working to birth Christ in us, in order that we might be conformed to his likeness. She loves and cares for us with persistence. Let's not let the devil rob us of her maternal care.

CHAPTER TWELVE

Marian Apparitions

Marian apparitions have been greatly misunderstood within Catholicism and without. This is likely due to exaggerations in devotion at a few apparition sites, in some cases even a fixation on Mary over and against Christ.

While living in southwest Florida, I drove past a small gathering of people in a parking lot. I realized that the building they were observing was one that had gained national attention due to an image of Mary clearly visible on its large window. This resembled the rainbow reflections of an oil spill when the sun hits just right. I called this image "oil-slick Mary."

I dare say that many people are not sure what to do with the supposed heavenly visitations that get reported now and then. Should we all take our candles and venerate a dinner roll that looks like Mother Teresa or a wall recently cleaned by a spray crew and left with a mysterious image of Jesus on it? This can't possibly be something the Church endorses, right?

At the time I saw the crowd in Florida, I wasn't aware of any ecclesial insights into what qualifies as a supernatural apparition. But I did conclude that if these images somehow led people into a genuine spirituality, then I wasn't opposed to them. Maybe God doesn't have anything to do with the image of Mary in a bread pan, but he can use the visual oddity to awaken spirituality in some people. Frederick Jelly, author of *Discerning the Miraculous*, seems to share that observation: "Here, it should be noted that an apparition need not be judged authentic in order to deepen the faith and devotion of individuals."[1]

What are we to do with images and apparitions then? Do we each come to a personal opinion about the matter at hand, or can we cling to something more substantial in deciphering them?

Means of Discernment

It must be noted from the outset that authentic Marian apparitions, messages, images, and other events possibly involving the supernatural can never present insights that contradict the deposit of faith. The Church serves and protects the Word of God in its written and oral, or traditional, form, and guaranteeing consistency in faith and morals is of the utmost importance. The Holy Spirit solidifies the consistency of Christ's words and deeds through the protective charism of infallibility, "whereby the pastors of the Church, the pope and bishops in union with him, can definitely proclaim a doctrine of faith or morals for the belief of the faithful" (*CCC*, Glossary).

Even Church-approved apparitions have their limitations. Jelly notes,

> The certitude that can be reached as a result of investigating apparitions and private revelations can never be the certitude of divine faith that we receive in the mysteries of the Trinity, the Incarnation, the Eucharist, the Immaculate Conception, the Assumption, Mary's perpetual virginity, our call to the beatific vision, the resurrection of the body.[2]

So how can we know how to handle claims of Marian apparitions? The Church is our guide, investigating apparitions "to ascertain whether the phenomena are truly beyond human explanation, lest that which was thought to be miraculous be later explained as the result of natural causes, with the result that our faith is exposed to ridicule."[3]

When an apparition becomes known and is of interest, the validation of it as authentic must come from the local bishop. He evaluates the evidence to make sure that an apparition actually happened, first of all. The person involved in the apparition is investigated as well, to determine if he or she is psychologically balanced, honest, moral, and respectful of the Church's authority. The messages are carefully examined in order to determine if they are in line with Church teaching. The bishop makes sure that money is not a motive for the apparition claim. The fruit of an apparition should be religious devotion, not hysteria.

The Church does not require belief in private revelations. It is up to individuals to apply the messages as they see fit, knowing the Church's approval guarantees only that the apparition is not in conflict with the deposit of faith.

The Church approved a number of Marian apparitions in the twentieth century. Fatima, Portugal, is the most famous one, and

I will discuss it in more detail later in this chapter. Bishop Pablo Antonio Vega approved an apparition at Cuapa, Nicaragua, on November 13, 1982. The 1981 apparition to young adults at Kibeho in Rwanda was approved by Bishop Augustin Misago on June 29, 2001. Gladys de Motta, on September 25, 1983, in San Nicolas, Argentina, witnessed an apparition, which was later approved by Bishop Domingo Castagna. Cardinal Jaime Sin vouched for the apparition of Mary to a group of soldiers in Manila in 1986, during the overthrow of President Ferdinand Marcos.

Other approved apparitions occurred in Beauraing, Belgium; Banneux, Belgium; Zeitoun, Egypt (approved by the Coptic Church); Betania, Venezuela; and Amsterdam. A related phenomenon is the weeping Mary statue in Syracuse, Italy, called a lacrimation. And at a convent in Akita, Japan, blood dripped from the hand of a three-foot wooden statue, from which a nun named Agnes heard Our Lady speak. Dozens more of such supernatural events have been reported though not yet approved.

Earlier approved apparitions include that of Our Lady of Guadalupe to St. Juan Diego in Mexico in 1531. This was an occasion for numerous conversions among the Aztec people. And pilgrims still flock to Lourdes, France, where Mary appeared to St. Bernadette in 1858 and where numerous healings have occurred.

The manner in which bishops format letters or documents to affirm or deny the supernatural origin and content of apparitions is very specific. When the bishop of the diocese of Niigata, John Shojiro Ito, affirmed the apparitions at Akita, Japan, in 1984, he stated:

After the investigation conducted up to the present day, I recognize the supernatural character of a series of mysterious events concerning the statue of the Holy Mother Mary which is found in the convent of the Institute of the Handmaids of the Sacred Heart of Jesus in the Holy Eucharist at Yuzawadai, Soegawa, Akita. I do not find in these events any elements which are contrary to Catholic faith and morals.

Consequently, I authorize, throughout the entire diocese, the veneration of the Holy Mother of Akita, while awaiting that the Holy See publishes definitive judgment on this matter.[4]

On the other hand, the archbishop of Denver, in March of 1994, stated that the "alleged apparitions of the Blessed Virgin Mary to Theresa Antonia Lopez are devoid of any supernatural origin," and he instructed the faithful to "refrain from participating in or promoting para-liturgical or liturgical services related to the alleged apparitions.... Furthermore, anyone encouraging devotion to these alleged apparitions in any way is acting contrary to my wishes as Archbishop of Denver."[5]

Our Lady of Fatima

I rush to examine the apparitions at Fatima, Portugal, since these are approved and valued by many of the faithful. Lucia de Jesus dos Santos was ten years old, and her cousins Francisco and Jacinta Marto were eight and seven years of age, the first time they saw the Blessed Mother, on May 13, 1917. Five more times that year—on June 13, July 13, August 15, September 13, and

October 13—the children saw "a beautiful lady clothed all in white."[6] The general themes of these apparitions were prayer—particularly the rosary—sacrifice and penance, conversion, and Communion of reparation on the five first Saturdays.

These encounters with the Blessed Mother changed the children individually and the world eventually. During the third apparition Our Lady said, "Sacrifice yourself for sinners, and say often, especially when you make some sacrifice: 'O Jesus, this is for love of you, for the conversion of sinners, and in reparation for the sins committed against the Immaculate Heart of Mary.'"[7]

The children learned other prayers from an angel and from Our Lady that are still recited today. For instance:

> My God,
> I believe, I adore, I trust and love thee.
> I ask pardon for those
> who do not believe, do not adore, do not trust, and do not
>   love thee!

Another is

> Most Holy Trinity, Father, Son, and Holy Spirit,
> I adore You profoundly and offer You
> the most precious Body, Blood, Soul and Divinity of Jesus
>   Christ,
> present in all the tabernacles of the world,
> in reparation for the outrages, sacrileges, and indifference
>   with which He Himself is offended.
> And through the infinite merits of His Most Sacred Heart

and of the Immaculate Heart of Mary,

I beg of You the conversion of poor sinners.[8]

And probably the most known prayer given these seers is the one many people recite after each decade of the rosary:

O my Jesus,

forgive us our sins,

save us from the fires of hell;

lead all souls to heaven,

especially those in most need of thy mercy.

Mary's requests for prayers and sacrifices for the conversion of sinners, her emphasis on the seriousness of sin (she showed the children visions of hell), along with the determination of these young people amid great opposition, bespoke the authenticity of the apparitions from the start. Then, on October 13, 1917, the "Miracle of the Sun" lent credibility to the apparitions for the thousands in attendance. One observer wrote, "The sun, whirling wildly, seemed all at once to loosen itself from the firmament and, blood red, advance threateningly upon the earth as if to crush us with its huge and fiery weight."[9]

Many people have studied the apparitions of Fatima, and many more have put into practice the requests of Our Lady. The erection of a chapel was completed on October 13, 1921, in honor of Our Lady's request. This was destroyed by disbelievers, but the foundation was quickly laid for another church, which still stands.

Visitors to Fatima reported many healings, and "on May 3, 1922, the bishop of Leiria nominated a Commission of Inquiry. In 1927 the Holy See granted the privilege of a Votive Mass at Fatima."[10] Since that time the Church has approved and demonstrated the authenticity of these apparitions.

The Final Analysis

We are certainly a people who have had amazing encounters with the supernatural. God, in his mercy and love, "became flesh and dwelt among us" (John 1:14), showing us that we are not beyond his interest or reach. It should come as no surprise then that heaven and its holy inhabitants continue to visit earth.

In today's hunger for a continued encounter with the one greater than ourselves, we must not jump first toward otherworldly encounters but rather seek daily encounters with God in prayer, Scripture, and especially in the Eucharist. Jelly writes, "The grace of God is operative in the ordinary events of life. Apparitions are extraordinary events, that is, not part of our daily lives; they illumine the 'ordinary' sacramental ways in which we are sanctified."[11] If any apparition or vision would usurp this emphasis or direct us away from these ordinary means of knowing his presence, then it would be of no use to us.

There are times when the Lord chooses to speak to us from a supernatural perspective, as demonstrated in the Fatima apparitions, but clearly even there grace is building on nature, not pitting the spiritual against the physical. We are blessed with the protection of the Church, to guide us in knowing what is worth our attention and what is not.

Our Lady will always bring us to the sacraments; she will never take us away from Christ. The Church will never affirm something that distracts us from this encounter with Jesus; rather she will welcome opportunities to avail us the graces of heaven.

CHAPTER THIRTEEN

Flowers for Mary

On May 13, 2006, we celebrated the Feast of Our Lady of Fatima. The day was perfect. That morning I graduated with my master's degree in theology from Franciscan University of Steubenville. Following this wonderful occasion, my family prepared for the next adventure of the day, the baptism of our new son, Joseph.

Our arrival at St. Peter Catholic Church was one of excitement and expectation. The kids packed into the front couple rows, dressed to the hilt and eager to remind all in attendance that they, too, were part of the beautiful occasion. Joseph became fully alive in Christ on this special day dedicated to Our Lady.

On arriving home for the reception and celebration, I was overwhelmed with joy at the generosity of our God. To be able to baptize my son during the month of May, which is traditionally dedicated to Our Lady, and on such an important Marian feast, was very satisfying. I truly believed that the baptism of our son that day made an impact upon all of us individually and upon the Church, too.

How will this little life affect the Church in years to come? Only the Lord knows. But we his parents have committed ourselves to bringing him to Jesus through Mary. We pray that he will make of everything a sacrifice for the conversion of sinners, as Our Lady of Fatima encouraged the young children to do.

The day progressed in waves of responsibility as I attended to our guests. Many families came and went, we enjoyed tons of food, and throughout it all my cap and gown remained hidden for the greater joy of new life and consecration to Jesus through Mary.

As the day crept into early afternoon, I walked outside to catch a bit of fresh air, check on our guests, and make sure the children were accounted for. It was then I noticed bright colorful flowers in the hands of the little ones. They were placing them in a small red Radio Flyer wheelbarrow, wheeling them over to the Mary statue that stands near the entrance to our home, and carefully laying the flowers at her feet.

It took a moment for me to realize that these flowers were being picked from the two small bushes on the edge of our property that I had been trying not to run over with the lawnmower for the previous four years. Recently my wife had mentioned how disappointing these plants had been. They were not producing the extravagant flowers that other bushes of their family generally reveal. Today though, the little bushes were giving every petal they could, through the searching hands of the children, in order to honor and venerate the Blessed Virgin Mary.

I almost yelled at the children to stop plucking the tiny flowers from the pathetic branches of these bushes. Hey, I had bought those plants and had continued to carefully mow around them even though it would have been easier to put them out of their misery. But suddenly I realized that this in fact was a worthy sacrifice, both for the bushes and for my wife and me. What if those small bushes' flowers every year produced only enough blossoms to place at the feet of the Blessed Virgin's statue? They would be fulfilling exactly what they were created for. And of course, the kids' thoughtfulness brought joy to my heart.

I realize it is a weak comparison, but we, as children of God, are to be satisfied with the purpose and beauty to which the Lord has called us. We are to be like those little children bringing the beauty of what is within our reach to the feet of the Blessed Mother.

It may be that everyone else in your field is more recognized, has more output—better "blossoms"—while all you have to offer is the daily grind of family life, with little or no recognition for the many sacrifices you make. It may be that your Father in heaven is the only one who realizes that your gifts and fruit will one day be entirely depleted for the honor of your commitment to him and the Blessed Virgin. She will not be outdone by your total sacrifice. I love that truth!

May 13, 2006, was Mary's day in a powerful way, but really our whole lives are to be given to Jesus through our complete abandonment to the Mother of God. We can be filled with joy as each blossom is plucked and placed at her feet, realizing that the barren plant that remains is far more beautiful in light of the placement of its sacrificial offering.

Remember the widow's mite (see Luke 21:1–4)? She had little to offer God in the world's eyes, yet the smallness of her gift turned the head of our Lord! Jesus pointed her out because her generosity was a total gift.

Isn't that how Jesus loved us? His gift was an innocent and childlike donation to the Father for our redemption, which in turn grants us the grace of pleasing the Father's heart. The Mother of God, in complete obedience to the Father's will, also became a little one, bringing the wounds and sacrifices of her mother's heart to the Father.

Do you remember the small boy who offered the loaves and fishes to Jesus upon the disciples' request (see John 6:5–14)? He gave what he had, and Jesus satisfied thousands. That great miracle would not have happened had the lad been selfish.

Look around, and realize that Jesus is inviting you to bring your flowers to the feet of his mother. This will be a beautiful expression of love that the Father will savor. You can do great things to please our God, even if the world considers your gifts and sacrifices to be insignificant.

I brought my child Joseph to the Father by laying him before the Blessed Mother. During my life I will do what I can so that my children have something beautiful to place before Our Lady. She will teach us all how to bring joy to the Father.

I delight in consecrating my family daily to Jesus through Mary. We want to truly love Christ as Mary did. Whenever I see a statue of the Blessed Virgin, I look up to her with affection, interested in her intercession, wanting to learn more about her son from the witness of her life. I pray that her patience and humility will become present in me, especially as I train my children in loving Christ. I have much to learn from her.

Let us all pray that we can bring the flowers of our life to Jesus through Mary.

CHAPTER FOURTEEN

My Big Conclusion

Well, think about it: You are called to be a saint, and God has granted you everything to guarantee this is going to happen. You have to want what he wants, though!

When we begin to see his plan for our lives and the reality of Mary's being there to help us succeed, then we become more confident on our journey to holiness. Mary's role in our spiritual quest is not secondary or incidental. God demonstrates how important she is by entrusting her with his Son. Jesus depended upon Mary from infancy and found solace in her presence at the cross. And the Holy Spirit was intimate with her, as demonstrated in the Annunciation and the Incarnation, as well as in the birthing of the Church at Pentecost. Mary has been involved in it all!

She wants to be invited into every part of your journey, too. If God has chosen to unite himself so closely to Our Lady, why wouldn't you want to do the same?

You can choose to follow Our Lady's lead in uniting yourself to God's mission, or you can do your own thing. You can walk with Christ or away from him. You can be like Mary or Judas.

That sounds a bit harsh, I know, but it really is your choice. God wants you to be like Mary and choose him. You can't be made to do the right thing, for if you were, it wouldn't be authentic.

I encourage you to be yourself, rest in Christ, and know that Mary is pouring the graces of her son on you even now.

. . .

GLOSSARY

Some of the terms I use in this book are probably not part of your everyday language, so here are some definitions.

Advocate: Helper. Mary is our advocate because she is in fact our mother, too. She petitions Christ on behalf of her children, as Esther petitioned King Ahasuerus on behalf of her people.

Assumption: A dogma of the Catholic Church, defined in 1950, that holds that Mary was taken into heaven body and soul. Mary's body did not suffer decay, since by virtue of the Immaculate Conception, it was never subject to the effects of sin (see *CCC*, #966, 974).

Consecration to Mary: A practice popularized by St. Louis de Montfort of giving one's best to God by giving one's all to the Blessed Mother. As God chose to come to us through Mary in the Person of Jesus Christ, so we go to him through the Blessed Mother—not because we have to but because it is fitting in imitating Our Lord.

When the Second Person of the Trinity became incarnate, he was found with Mary. Jesus is the perfect son. We know as children of God that we must imitate him in all things, including Marian devotion and veneration. We strive to give her every heartbeat, breath, involuntary and voluntary action, moment, and indulgence or possible indulgence, so that we can be her loving servants and servants of God.

If you are interested in being consecrated to Mary, you should read *True Devotion to the Blessed Virgin Mary* by St. Louis de Montfort.

Deposit of Faith: The Church's heritage, contained in sacred Scripture and Tradition. Within God's revelation to humanity, Jesus reveals the Father in the love of the Holy Spirit. This encounter of humanity with divinity is extended through Jesus' establishing of the kingdom of God. He sends the Holy Spirit, who reminds the apostles of all that Jesus said and did. This full revelation in Christ, given to the apostles in the love of the Spirit, cannot be added to but has been unfolded over time.

Divine Revelation: God's Word, expressed through sacred Scripture and Tradition and conveying to the world God's love. The magisterium of the Catholic Church is the servant, a consistent interpretive voice, of this divine revelation.

Doctrine: "Any truth taught by the Church as necessary for acceptance by the faithful. The truth may be either formally revealed (as the real presence), or a theological conclusion (as the canonization of a saint), or part of the natural law (as the sinfulness of contraception). In any case, what makes it doctrine is that the Church authority teaches that it is to be believed."[1]

Dogma: "The Church's Magisterium exercises the authority it holds from Christ to the fullest extent when it defines dogmas, that is, when it proposes, in a form obliging the Christian people to an irrevocable adherence of faith, truths contained in divine

Revelation or also when it proposes, in a definitive way, truths having a necessary connection with these" (*CCC*, #88).

Immaculate Conception: The dogma, proclaimed on December 8, 1854, that Mary was without original or actual sin, completely free to submit to the Father's will. She is totally with her Son in enmity with the Serpent and his seed (see Genesis 3:15; *CCC*, #491, 492).

Magisterium: The teaching office of the Catholic Church, comprising the bishops in communion with the pope. The magisterium preserves a consistent interpretation of the Word of God in both its written and living tradition.

Mediatrix of All Graces: A title for Mary, in virtue of her willing collaboration with and under Jesus for our redemption. By the merits of Christ, Mary has the opportunity to distribute the fruits of this redemption to the body of Christ (see *CCC*, #970).

Mysteries of the Rosary: Twenty events from the life of Christ upon which we meditate in saying the rosary. There are four primary themes: the joyful, luminous, sorrowful, and glorious mysteries. Within each group are five mysteries to be meditated upon.

- Within the **Joyful**: the Annunciation, the Visitation, the Nativity, the presentation of the child Jesus in the temple, and the finding of Jesus in the temple.
- The **Luminous**: the baptism of Jesus, the wedding feast at Cana, the proclamation of the kingdom of God, the Transfiguration, and the institution of the Eucharist.

- The **Sorrowful**: the agony in the garden, the scourging at the pillar, the crowning with thorns, the carrying of the cross, and the crucifixion.
- And finally the **Glorious** mysteries: the Resurrection, the Ascension, the descent of the Holy Spirit, the Assumption, and the crowning of Mary as Queen of Heaven.

Original Sin: Adam and Eve's sin of disobedience, which deprived humanity of grace (see *CCC*, #390, 397, 398). This deprivation of grace is remedied by our baptism into the life of Christ. We are taken out of the family of Satan and placed into the family of God.

Mary was never deprived of this grace in any way; she was never on the side of the Serpent. She was preserved from original sin through the Immaculate Conception. This preservative redemption is one of Christ's great salvific effects.

Perpetual Virginity: Mary's "virginal integrity" before, during, and after the birth of Jesus. She is the living ark of the covenant and the pure and unblemished new Eve (see *CCC*, #496–507, 510).

Theotokos: "Bearer of God." Church dogma holds Mary to be the Mother of God because Jesus is fully God and fully man (see *CCC*, #495).

Typology: The discernment of events and persons in the Old Testament as signs pointing to that which is greater in the New. The New Testament is concealed in the Old, and the Old is revealed in the New (see *CCC*, #129–130).

. . .

NOTES

CHAPTER TWO: *Mary the Woman*

1. See Vatican II, *Dei Verbum*, Dogmatic Constitution on Divine Revelation, 11.

2. Mark Shea, www.mark-shea.com.

3. Richard A. Batey, *New Testament Nuptial Imagery* (Leiden, Netherlands: E.J. Brill, 1971), p. 13.

4. Jean Guitton, *The Virgin Mary* (New York: P.J. Kenedy, 1952), p. 20.

5. John Paul II, *Vita Consecrata*, Post-Synodal Apostolic Exhortation on the Consecrated Life and Its Mission in the Church and in the World, 34, March 25, 1996, www.vatican.va.

6. Guitton, p. 22.

7. Guitton, p. 22.

8. Guitton, p. 23.

9. Guitton, p. 24.

10. Vatican II, *Nostra Aetate*, Declaration on the Relation of the Church to Non-Christian Religions, 1.

11. Within God's self-revelation, partially through the economy of salvation (the way God reveals himself to people in time), humanity catches a glimpse of who he is (*theologia*). The more

we understand God's inner essence, the greater our lucidity regarding his *oikonomia*, the way he speaks to us through what he's created (see *CCC*, #236). For further study on the economy of salvation, check out Scott Hahn, *A Father Who Keeps His Promises: God's Covenant Love in Scripture* (Ann Arbor, Mich.: Servant, 1998).

CHAPTER THREE: *Mary and the Trinity*

1. David Supple, *Virgin Wholly Marvelous* (Cambridge, Mass.: Ravengate, 1991), p. ix, quoting Gerard Manley Hopkins.
2. For more on this, see Hahn.
3. Paul VI, *Signum Magnum*, Apostolic Exhortation to the Catholic Bishops of the World, pt. 2, no. 2, May 13, 1967, www.vatican.va.
4. See Vatican II, *Lumen Gentium*, Dogmatic Constitution on the Church, 53; National Conference of Catholic Bishops, *Behold Your Mother: Woman of Faith*, 53, November 10, 1973 (Washington, D.C.: USCC, 1973).
5. See *Lumen Gentium*, 62.
6. Maximilian Kolbe, letter to Fr. Salezy Mikolajczyk, July 28, 1935, as quoted in H.M. Manteau-Bonamy, *Immaculate Conception and the Holy Spirit: The Marian Teachings of St. Maximilian Kolbe*, Richard Arnandez, trans. (Libertyville, Ill.: Marytown, 2008), p. 40.
7. Pope Paul VI, *Signum Magnum*, pt. 1.
8. Ewert Cousins, Introduction to Bonaventure, *The Soul's Journey Into God, The Tree of Life, The Life of St. Francis*, The Classics of Western Spirituality (Mahwah, N.J.: Paulist, 1978), pp. 25–26.

CHAPTER FOUR: *Four Fabulous Dogmas*

1. See Dogmatic Definition of the Council of Chalcedon, 451, www.ewtn.com.

2. See George Johnson, Jerome D. Hannan, and Dominica Johnson, *The Story of the Church: Her Founding, Mission and Progress* (New York: Benzinger, 1935), p. 97.

3. Augustine, as quoted in David Supple, p. 2.

4. Pope Pius IX, *Defining the Dogma of the Immaculate Conception: Ineffabilis Deus* (Boston: St. Paul, 1992), p. 14.

CHAPTER FIVE: *Trailblazer for Heroic Spirituality*

1. *Lumen Gentium*, 62.

2. "The Church…has illuminated the unity of the divine plan in the two Testaments through typology, which discerns in God's works of the Old Covenant prefigurations of what he accomplished in the fullness of time in the person of his incarnate Son" (*CCC*, #128).

3. *Lumen Gentium*, 65.

CHAPTER SIX: *The Ecumenical Mary*

1. M.J. Sheeben, *Mariology*, T.L.M.J. Geukers, trans. (New York: Herder, 1946), vol. 1, p. 10.

2. Sheeben, pp. 11–12.

CHAPTER SEVEN: *Saint for the Saints*

1. "St. Maximilian Kolbe, Priest Hero of a Death Camp," pamphlet quoted at www.catholicpages.com.

2. C.S. Lewis, *The Weight of Glory* (New York: Macmillan, 1965), pp. 18–19.

CHAPTER EIGHT: *The Rosary: An Introduction*

1. Pope John Paul II, *Rosarium Virginis Mariae*, Apostolic Letter on the Most Holy Rosary, 1, October 16, 2002, www.vatican.va.

2. Pope Pius V, as quoted in Supple, p. 131.

3. Pope Leo XIII, *Supremi Apostolatus Officio*, Encyclical on Devotion of the Rosary, 5, September 1, 1883, www.vatican.va.

4. Pope Leo XIII, as quoted in Supple, p. 132.

5. Pope Leo XIII, as quoted in Supple, p. 132.

6. Louis de Montfort, as quoted at www.communityof hopeinc.org.

CHAPTER TEN: *Mary at Mass*

1. Vatican II, *Sacrosanctum Concilium*, The Constitution on the Sacred Liturgy, 14.

2. Excerpt from "The Fifteen Prayers of St. Bridget of Sweden," as quoted at http://fisheaters.com.

3. William Thomas Walsh, *Our Lady of Fatima* (Garden City, N.Y.: Image, 1955), pp. 41–42.

CHAPTER ELEVEN: *The Attack*

1. Pope John Paul II, *Familiaris Consortio*, Apostolic Exhortation on the Role of the Christian Family in the Modern World, 23, November 22, 1981, www.vatican.va.

2. Cardinal Joseph Ratzinger with Vittorio Messori, *The Ratzinger Report: An Exclusive Interview on the State of the Church* (San Francisco: Ignatius, 1985), pp. 98, 99.

CHAPTER TWELVE: *Marian Apparitions*

1. Frederick M. Jelly, *Discerning the Miraculous: Norms for Judging Apparitions and Private Revelations,* vol. 44, *Marian Studies* (Dayton: Mariological Society of America, 1993), p. 50.

2. Jelly, p. 44.

3. Jelly, p. 50.

4. John Shojiro Ito, Bishop of Niigata, Japan, April 22, 1984, as quoted at www.miraclehunter.com.

5. Archbishop J. Francis Stafford, Declaration Concerning Alleged Apparitions of the Blessed Virgin Mary at Mother Cabrini Shrine and Other Places in the Archdiocese, Denver, March 9, 1994, quoted at www.miraclehunter.com.

6. Peter Heintz, *A Guide to Apparitions of our Blessed Virgin Mary* (Sacramento, Calif.: Gabriel, 1995), p. 23.

7. Heintz, p. 26.

8. Walsh, pp. 41–42.

9. "The Miracle of the Sun: An Eyewitness Account by Dr. José Maria de Almeida Garrett, Professor at the Faculty of Sciences of Coimbra, Portugal," www.fatima.org. Dr. Garrett's full account may be found in *Novos Documentos de Fatima* (San Paulo: Loyola, 1984).

10. Heintz, p. 36.

11. Jelly, p. 50.

GLOSSARY

1. John A. Hardon, *Pocket Catholic Dictionary* (New York: Image, 1985), p. 117.

About the Author

Chris Padgett is an author, singer, songwriter, and international speaker. He has a master's degree in theology from Franciscan University of Steubenville and is completing his doctoral degree with an emphasis in Marian studies from the International Marian Research Institute in Dayton, Ohio. He is the author of *Spirituality You Can Live With: Stronger Faith in 30 Days*. He coauthored with his wife, Linda, *Not Ready for Marriage, Not Ready for Sex: One Couple's Return to Chastity*.

Chris and Linda are the parents of nine children and live in Steubenville, Ohio. You can find out more about their ministries at www.chrispadgett.com.